CW01064879

Multimedia
Made Simple

990502432 8

Made Simple *Computer Books*

● easy to follow ● jargon free ● practical ● task based ● easy steps

Thousands of people have already discovered that the **MADE SIMPLE** series gives them what they want *fast!* These are the books for you if you want to **learn quickly what's essential** and **how** to do things with a particular piece of software. You are:

● **a Secretary** or **temp** who wants to **get the job done**, **quickly** and **efficiently**

● **a Manager**, without the time to learn all about the software but who wants to **produce** letters, **memos, reports** or **spreadsheets**

● someone **working from home**, who needs a **self-teaching** approach, that gives **results fast**, with the least confusion.

For **clarity** and **simplicity**, the **MADE SIMPLE** Computer Books stand above all others.

This **best selling** series is in your **local bookshop now**, or in case of difficulty, contact:

Reed Book Services Ltd., Orders Dept, PO Box 5, Rushden, Northants, NN10 9YX.
Tel 0933 58521. Fax 0933 50284. Credit card sales 0933 410511.

Series titles:

Excel for Windows	Stephen Morris	0 7506 2070 6	
Lotus 1-2-3 (DOS)	Ian Robertson	0 7506 2066 8	
MS-DOS	Ian Sinclair	0 7506 2069 2	
MS-Works for Windows	P. K. McBride	0 7506 2065 X	
Windows 3.1	P. K. McBride	0 7506 2072 2	
Word for Windows	Keith Brindley	0 7506 2071 4	
WordPerfect (DOS)	Stephen Copestake	0 7506 2068 4	
Access for Windows	Moira Stephen	0 7506 2309 8	
The Internet	P.K.McBride	0 7506 2308 X	
Quicken for Windows	Stephen Copestake	0 7506 2311 X	
WordPerfect for Windows	Keith Brindley	0 7506 2310 1	
Lotus 123 (5.0) for Windows	Stephen Morris	0 7506 2307 1	
Multimedia	Simon Collin	0 7506 2314 4	
Pageplus for Windows	Ian Sinclair	0 7506 2312 8	
Powerpoint	Moira Stephen	0 7506 2420 5	
Harddisk Management	Ian Sinclair	0 7506 2421 3	October '95
Windows 95	P.K. McBride	0 7506 2306 3	October '95
AmiPro for Windows	Moira Stephen	0 7506 2067 6	October '95
Microsoft Office	P.K. McBride	0 7506 2306 3	October '95

Multimedia
Made Simple

Simon Collin

Made Simple
BOOKS

Made Simple
An imprint of Butterworth-Heinemann Ltd
Linacre House, Jordan Hill, Oxford OX2 8DP

  R   A member of the Reed Elsevier plc group

OXFORD   LONDON   BOSTON
MUNICH   NEW DELHI   SINGAPORE   SYDNEY
TOKYO   TORONTO   WELLINGTON

First published 1995
© Simon Collin 1995

All rights reserved. No part of this publication
may be reproduced in any material form (including
photocopying or storing in any medium by electronic
means and whether or not transiently or incidentally
to some other use of this publication) without the
written permission of the copyright holder except in
accordance with the provisions of the Copyright,
Design and Patents Act 1988 or under the terms of a
licence issued by the Copyright Licensing Agency Ltd,
90 Tottenham Court Road, London, England W1P 9HE.
Applications for the copyright holder's written permission
to reproduce any part of this publication should be addressed
to the publishers

TRADEMARKS/REGISTERED TRADEMARKS
Computer hardware and software brand names mentioned in this book are protected
by their respective trademarks and are acknowledged.

British Library Cataloguing in Publication Data
A catalogue record for this book is available from the British Library

ISBN 0 7506 2314 4

Typeset by P.K.McBride, Southampton

Archtype, Bash Casual, Cotswold and Gravity fonts from Advanced Graphics Ltd
Icons designed by Sarah Ward © 1994
Printed and bound in Great Britain

GLOUCESTERSHIRE
COUNTY LIBRARY
Class
Copy

Contents

Preface

Welcome to Multimedia Made Simple. Multimedia is the most exciting area of computing at the moment and it's also great fun to experiment with. This book explains everything you need to know to get started in multimedia. How the different parts work, how to use them and what to do with them. We also cover how to create your own multimedia titles: from an interactive catalogue to simple sounds in a memo.

Multimedia software is all the rage: exciting games, animations, encyclopaedias, all available on a CD-ROM. This book shows you how to install commercial software, how to use the software and how to tune your PC so that the software will really fly!

All the complex hardware and software components are explained and we'll show you how to upgrade your PC to take advantage of multimedia.

If you are interested in multimedia, Multimedia Made Simple is a painless way of getting into the subject. It was great fun to write, and I hope it makes multimedia just as fun for you to learn about.

1 Introducing Multimedia

The Jargon

Like all sections of computing, multimedia is packed with jargon. What's worse is that since the technology is still developing, the jargon changes with it. In this section are described the basic terms that make up multimedia and will help you get going with the rest of this book.

Multimedia

Multimedia is any software or presentation that combines different media: sound, video, images, and text. You can buy multimedia applications (for example, that describe with pictures, spoken commentary and video how the human body works or how computers work) or you can create your own presentations and applications.

The screenshot below is from Encarta, an example of Multimedia at its best.

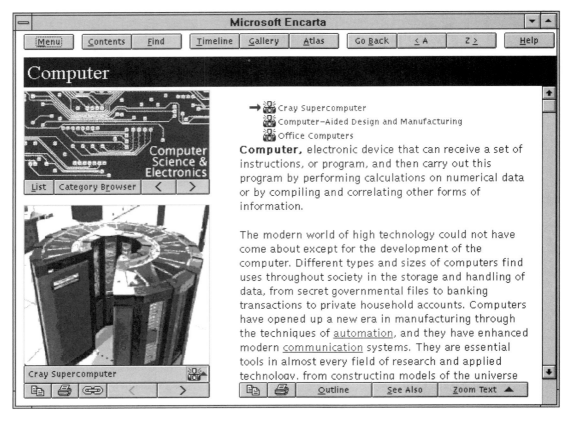

Take note

There is a glossary of Multimedia terms at the back of this book.

Hypertext

Multimedia applications often have hypertext links. A hypertext link is a special word, button or picture that, if you click on it, will move you to another page or display a piece of text. It's often used to show more detail about a particular topic. The special words with links to another page are normally described as *hot-words* or *hotlinks* and are displayed in a different colour. If you move the mouse pointer over a hotword, it changes shape to look like a hand.

Page

Multimedia applications are normally made up of pages. Each page is really a screen-full of information. If you are creating your own multimedia application, you can place text, buttons, images, sound or video clips on each page then link the pages together so that a user can move through the '*book*' (the name for a complete multimedia application with several pages).

Button

A button is a little icon on screen that normally starts something if you click on it. Simple buttons are just square outlines, others have shading to make them look three-dimensional. Buttons can start a video or sound clip or move to another page.

Video clip

A video clip is sequence of images that are displayed rapidly to give the impression of movement. To give smooth motion, your PC needs to display over 25 frames every second - each frame is a separate image, so even a short video clip takes up a huge amount of space on your disk. If you want to record video clips from a video camera or television, you'll need special hardware to plug into your PC. If you want to play back a video sequence, you don't need any special hardware.

Take note

To capture data from outside your PC you will need to add special hardware: a scanner for images, a video camera for video and a microphone for sounds.

Still from a video clip

Sound

Your PC can play simple beeps through its speaker or, by adding a sound card, you can record and play back stereo CD-quality sound or control electronic drum machines and synthesizers.

Images

With a high-resolution colour monitor you can display life-like images and edit them using paint software.

The visible aspect of sound

IconAuthor (opposite) is a powerful authoring package that lets you create multimedia titles.

What is Multimedia?

❑ In this book you will see how these technologies work, how to control them and how, with the tools built into Windows 3.1, to use them in your own applications to make memos more exciting, presentations more eye-catching or create your own interactive software.

There is a lot of confusion about what exactly is multimedia. It is a presentation, game or application that combines different media. Your computer can use video clips, sound recordings, images, animation and text, and can control external devices such as a video recorder, video disc player, CD-ROM drive, synthesizer and video camera.

If the program plays a sequence of sound, video and images, this is *multimedia*. If the program lets the user control the sequence by selecting different options, it is called *interactive multimedia*.

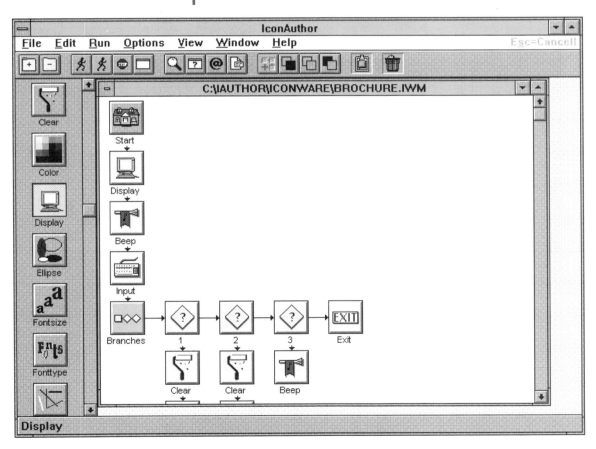

Using Multimedia

Over the next few pages, you will see what extra hardware you need to install in your PC to allow it to run multimedia titles that you can buy from computer shops.

Developing Your Own Multimedia

Multimedia is one of the most creative areas of computing because you don't need to be an experienced programmer to create an application. It's easy for a user to create a simple presentation: once you have mastered recording sounds, editing images and blending these together, you will be able to tackle simple authoring tools that let any non-programmer create stunning results.

The screenshot below is taken from Scoremaster, a powerful but simple-to-use sound sequencer and editing program.

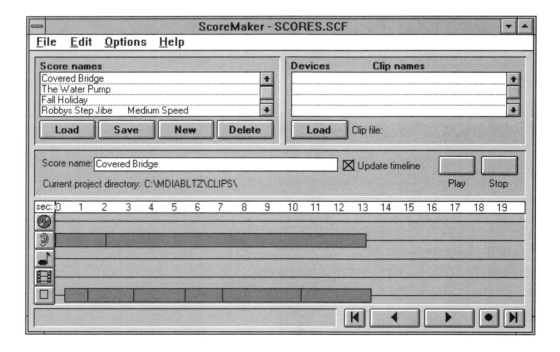

Multimedia and Windows

The multimedia revolution hit the PC with the release of Microsoft Windows 3.1. This is the simple-to-use graphical front-end to DOS that a user can control with a mouse. What makes Windows 3.1 or Windows for Workgroups special is that it has all the functions and tools you need to get started with multimedia built into to it. Windows lets you access any CD-ROM drive, move files to hard disk and play back sound, video or animation files.

Windows includes utilities that let you record sounds onto your hard disk then edit them or add special effects. It lets you play back video clips, paint images and control external equipment including synthesizers, video discs and music CDs.

Sound Recorder

Sound Recorder

This utility controls the sound card installed in your multimedia PC. Through Sound Recorder, you can record sounds, edit them, add effects then play them back in stereo, CD-quality.

Media Player

Media Player

This controls the remaining multimedia devices connected to your PC, for example, a video disc or audio CD. It can also play back multimedia files including video clips, sound recordings, animation sequences or MIDI music files.

File Manager

File Manager

Once you have installed a CD-ROM drive in your PC, you can access it through the File Manager program. It's also useful if you are installing commercial software from a CD-ROM or if you want to copy clip-art or other files from a CD-ROM onto your hard disk.

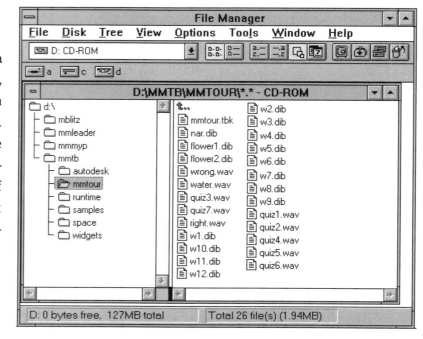

Paintbrush

Paintbrush

This utility lets you create your own images. You can edit existing images, or paint and draw images to use as a background to an application, or design your own icons or buttons.

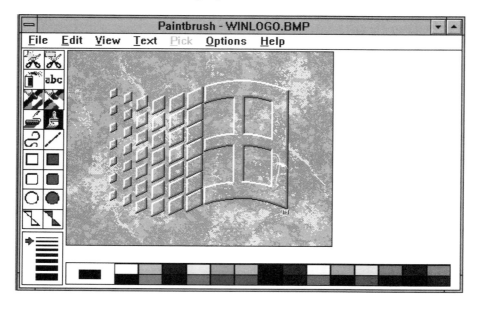

2 Multimedia Hardware

The equipment

Before you can start to use the multimedia features of Windows, or run a multimedia application, you must install the correct hardware on your PC. If you bought a multimedia-ready PC then you should have everything you need - but it is still worth reading the next few pages to make sure that you understand what each new piece of hardware does.

To get going with multimedia, your PC should have:

Sound Card

This plugs into an expansion slot in your PC and converts digital data from the PC into sound - it also lets you record sounds onto your hard disk.

CD-ROM drive

This should be next on your shopping list. The drive is the device into which you place the CD-ROM disc; it also needs a special controller card that fits into an expansion slot in your PC. You can use the CD-ROM drive to access commercial applications that are on CD-ROM or to play normal audio CDs. You cannot save your own files onto a CD-ROM (the acronym stands for Read Only Memory).

If you are a keen photographer, you can use your CD-ROM drive to access PhotoCD discs. When you send your film in to be developed, you can ask the laboratory to make a PhotoCD (a special type of CD-ROM) on which are stored high-resolution colour scans of your photographs.

Take note

More adventurous users might want to eventually add a scanner to capture images or a video camera and capture card to record video sequences.

Memory

Make sure that your PC has enough main memory (RAM). You will need a minimum of 4Mb to run Windows and 8Mb is recommended if you are likely to edit large images or video clips. (See page 22 to find out how to check your RAM).

Graphics Adapter

Last on the list is the graphics adapter. This is either built into the main electronics of your PC or is supplied as a card that fits into an expansion slot. In order to display high-resolution images in colour you will need a graphics adapter. The current standard is S-VGA; if you have an older VGA adapter you should be able to run most multimedia software - but check before you buy it.

The MPC Specification

To make it easier for anyone trying to buy the right PC with all the extras required for multimedia, there is a set of specifications that define the minimum requirements for any PC that claims to be able to run multimedia applications. It's called the MPC specification and provides a good starting point if you are trying to assess a new PC.

If a PC is MPC compliant it will have an official sticker that proves this and will let you run most multimedia titles.

An advancement of the MPC standard is called MPC-2; this lets you display higher quality images and record clearer sound.

The CD-ROM drive

A CD-ROM disc is a small plastic-coated disc that holds information as tiny holes in a central metal layer. It looks and works just like a normal audio CD. A laser beam is used to 'read' the holes in the disc as it spins in the drive.

To spin the disc and control the laser you need a CD-ROM drive and to interface the CD-ROM drive to your PC you need a controller card. Some sound cards have a CD-ROM controller built-in, otherwise you will need a special card called a SCSI card (see page 14 on how to install a card).

CD-ROM drives can either be fitted inside your PC in one of the free 5 1/4-inch drive bays in the front panel or can be fitted externally. External drives have their own case and power supply and are useful if you need to share a drive between PCs - but they still need a controller card in each PC.

At the front of all CD-ROM drives is an access slot for the disc. There are two ways of inserting the disc, which vary according to the drive. Some manufacturers use a caddy: you fit the disc inside the plastic caddy (which looks rather like a CD case) and then slide the whole lot inside the drive. Other drives use a tray - like an audio CD player; a motorised tray slides out from the drive and you place the disc on top and push it back into place.

Take note

A **CD-ROM** can store **650Mb** of data: the data can be audio, video, text or images.

Free drive bay for CD-ROM drive

Front view of your PC

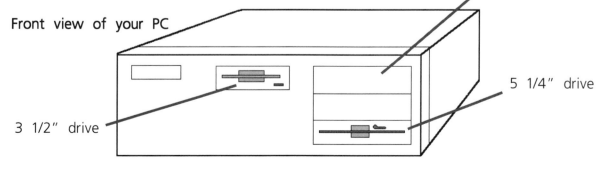

3 1/2" drive

5 1/4" drive

Front view of CD-ROM drive

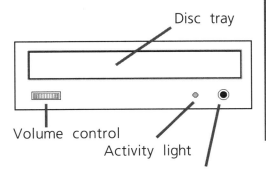

Disc tray

Volume control

Activity light

Headphone socket

Below the disc access slot is a socket for a pair of headphones, together with a volume control. Almost all CD-ROM drives can play audio CDs which you can listen to by plugging in a pair of headphones. You control the play, stop and fast-forward functions from the Media Player utility in Windows.

Tip

When handling a disc, try not to touch the surface. Hold it by the edge or in the central hole. Always store discs in their box to avoid dust and scratches. If you need to clean a very dirty disc, wipe it with a lint-free cloth with movements from the central hole out to the edge - not around the disc.

Buying Decisions

The speed of a disc drive is measured by its access time: a fast drive has an access time of less than 250msec. This describes how fast data can be located on the disc. A second measure describes how fast the data is then transferred to the PC: a quad-speed drive transfers data at four times the speed of an older drive by spinning the disc four-times faster. If you're playing video titles the speed of the drive will effect the quality of the video playback.

In order to use a PhotoCD disc (which can store photo-graphic images) you will need to make sure that your CD-ROM drive is multi-session compatible. If it is a CD-ROM/XA drive then it can read XA discs that hold both video and audio data.

The sound card

A sound card fits inside your PC into an expansion slot and converts digital data from the PC into sound waves which you can listen to by plugging a pair of speakers into the sound card. The card can also work in reverse and record any sound from a microphone by converting it into data which can be stored on your hard disk.

Recording Sound

The card works by a process called sampling. A sound wave is an analogue signal - a constantly changing signal. Unfortunately, a computer cannot handle these signals, since it can only manage numerical data, and so it has to convert the sound into a number form.

The card does this by looking at the level of the voice signal repeatedly (actually several thousand times every second) and noting the level of the signal at that time. This converts the signal into a stream of numbers that describe its height as it varies with time. It's these numbers that are be stored on disk.

Playing Sound

Playing back a sound normally works in exactly the reverse to recording: the computer passes a stream of numbers to the card which turns these into an analogue signal by changing the level according to the number, amplifies the signal and plays this through the speakers.

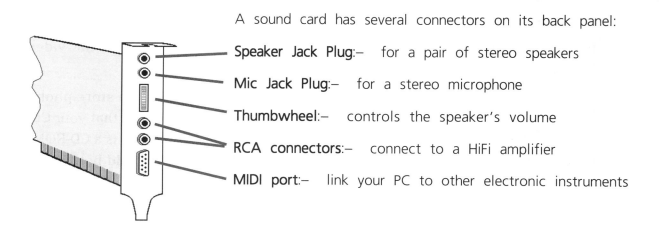

A sound card has several connectors on its back panel:

Speaker Jack Plug:– for a pair of stereo speakers

Mic Jack Plug:– for a stereo microphone

Thumbwheel:– controls the speaker's volume

RCA connectors:– connect to a HiFi amplifier

MIDI port:– link your PC to other electronic instruments

Volume

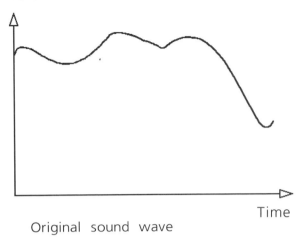

Time

Original sound wave

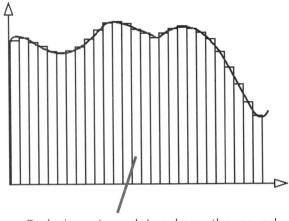

Each is a 'sample', where the sound card measures the level of the signal

Sample Rate

To record fine detail in the signal, the card has to be able to sample very fast. This can generate a huge amount of data, so you have a trade-off between the amount of data and the accuracy of the recording. For normal voice recordings, you need a card that can sample at 8KHz (8,000 times per second), for high-quality audio you should use 16KHz and for studio-quality sound 24KHz is a must.

Sample Size

The sample rate is only part of the story: the second factor that effects quality is the size of the sample word. For example, many sound cards use an 8-bit sample word; each sample is stored within 8 bits and so can be one of 256 different numbers or levels. For a more accurate representation of a signal you need to distinguish between finer levels in the samples; a 16-bit sample can differentiate between 64,000 levels but takes twice as much space on the disk as an 8-bit sample.

MIDI

Sound cards almost always have a MIDI port. This is a high-speed serial port used to connect your PC to electronic musical instruments, such as a keyboard or drum machine. Windows includes utilities that let you record the notes played on a drum machine and play them back later.

A Synthesizer

For more sophisticated musical effects, you can control external electronic instruments using the MIDI interface on your sound card. You can plug in up to 32 instruments such as a keyboard, drum machine, or synthesizer.

The MIDI port transmits musical notes to each instrument, or record notes from each instrument to the PC. It can also select special effects: for example, the controlling software on your PC could select a tin-drum and then send a series of notes, change to a piano effect and send the same series of notes. The software can also record notes played on an instrument, so the PC can act as a type of digital tape recorder.

Other features

Your sound card might also contain a waveform synthesizer chip. This is another way of creating sounds using a set of pre-recorded noises stored in a chip on the card. The music software controls how the noises are mixed together to create new sounds.

Tip

Some sound cards are advertised as 16-bit cards, but this might only refer to the fact that they fit in a 16-bit slot rather than record 16-bit samples. Make sure that you now exactly what you're buying!

The screen display

Buying Tips

The quality of a monitor is described by its dot-pitch. This is a measure of how fine the individual pixels on the screen are: the smaller this number, the sharper the image.

A local bus graphics adapter is a good choice if you intend to do a lot of image or video editing; the local bus is a very fast expansion bus fitted to high-performance PCs.

Tip

If you want to display what's on your computer monitor on a normal TV set, you'll need a genlock device.

In order to display anything on your screen (an image or video clip) your PC needs a *graphics adapter* that fits into an expansion slot - or is integrated as part of the PC's main electronics. The card controls the individual pixels - the tiny points on a screen - that make up a character or image. To display colours, the brightness of three colours (red, green and blue) pixels is varied and, to your eye, they combine to look like a colour.

Almost all new PCs come fitted with a graphics card that can support the VGA standard. This allows images of up to 640x480 pixels to be displayed in up to 64,000 colours. Watch out, because many commercial multimedia software now requires better graphics than VGA, normally the S-VGA standard that increases the resolution to 800x600 pixels.

In order to display the output from a graphics adapter you need a monitor that is capable of supporting the correct resolution. If you are upgrading your graphics adapter, make sure that the monitor can support the resolution of the card.

Graphics Adapter RAM

The graphics adapter has its own memory area on the card that is used to store the image that's being displayed. Many cards allow you to increase the amount of RAM fitted to the graphics adapter - and this will immediately increase the number of colours or the resolution that the card can display.

Image capture

Video Cameras

If you are feeling adventurous - and rich - you can expand your PC to allow it to capture video clips from a video camera, TV or VCR. The video capture card stores around 25 frames of images every second. Since each frame is a complete colour image, storing video takes up a vast amount of disk space: for example, 10 seconds of video could easily take up 2-3Mb of disk space.

Video playback

You do not need special hardware in order to play back video clips on your PC. Video clips are stored in a compressed format to save space with an AVI file extension. The Windows Media Player utility will let you play back video clips.

> **Take note**
>
> Within Windows, the standard way of storing video clips is the AVI (Audio-Visual Interleaved) format. These files contain both sound and video, and their filenames have an .AVI extension.

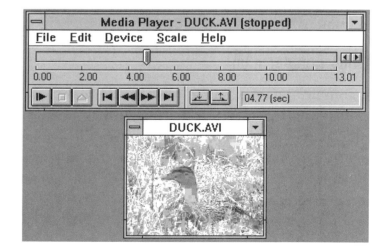

Windows Media Player is a simple but effective video playback system; here the video sequence is displayed in a small window below the control panel.

A Scanner

A scanner is very useful if you want to import logos, images or graphics into your PC. For simple work, a hand-held scanner provides a cheap way to import images. For more accurate work, or for better definition, a flat-bed scanner is recommended.

A scanner works rather like a photocopier: it shines a light onto the paper to be scanned and a light-sensitive head passes over the image detecting the light reflected from the image. This is then converted into a form which can be displayed in a paint or drawing package.

A hand-held scanner normally comes with its own interface card that fits into an expansion slot of your PC. A flat-bed scanner normally connects to a SCSI controller card; if you have a CD-ROM drive you probably already have a SCSI controller into which you can plug the scanner

Take note

Scanners convert a picture into a series of tiny dots; the number of dots depends upon the resolution of the scanner. 300 dots per inch is normal and is good enough for printing on a laser printer.

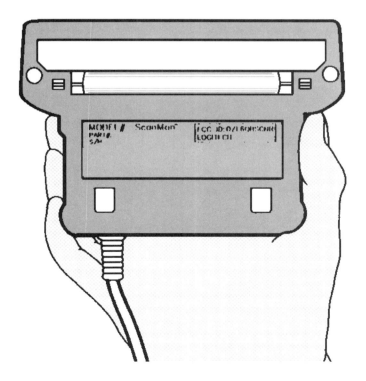

Light strip
Roller

Tip

Hand held scanners offer a cheap and easy way to import line drawings and black & white images.

Summary

❏ **Multimedia** is the use of a combination of sound, text, video and graphics

❏ Windows includes many **utilities** to control multimedia devices and play back sound or video clips

❏ For a **good setup**, your PC needs at least 4Mb of RAM, a CD-ROM player, sound card and a colour S-VGA monitor

❏ The **higher the quality** of sound recorded, the **more disk space** it needs

❏ More **advanced systems** can control video discs, video cameras and synthesizers

3 Upgrading your PC

Installing new hardware

Many users will have to upgrade one or more components in their PC to take advantage of the multimedia functions in Windows or to use a multimedia title.

Some users will need to add just a sound card, others should increase the RAM in their PC. If you have a very basic PC, then you might have to install a CD-ROM, sound card and more RAM. This chapter shows you how to check which parts of your PC need to be upgraded and how to install the new hardware.

What do I need to upgrade?

If you want to use commercial multimedia titles, you will need a CD-ROM drive. (See page 12). Do you have a CD-ROM drive?

For almost all multimedia applications, you'll need a sound card. (See page 14). Do you have a sound card?

Your PC will need at least 4Mb of RAM fitted. If you are planning to use video or do a lot of image editing, you should increase this to at least 8Mb. Double-click on the MS-DOS icon and, at the C:\> prompt, type in the command 'MEM'. This will tell you the total memory installed. Do you have 4Mb fitted?

Tip

If you have a multimedia-ready PC or a PC that conforms to the MPC standard, then you can skip this chapter and get straight onto experimenting with multimedia.

MS-DOS
Prompt

Checking RAM memory with DOS's MEM command. This PC is fitted with 8Mb – as shown in the line 'Total Memory'.

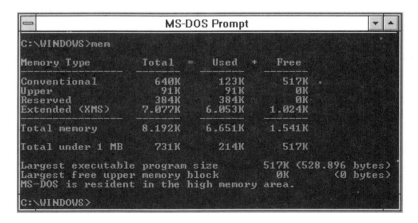

```
                              MS-DOS Prompt

C:\WINDOWS>mem

Memory Type         Total  =    Used   +    Free
                    ─────       ─────       ─────
Conventional         640K        123K        517K
Upper                 91K         91K          0K
Reserved             384K        384K          0K
Extended (XMS)     7.077K      6.053K       1.024K
                   ─────       ─────        ─────
Total memory       8.192K      6.651K       1.541K

Total under 1 MB     731K        214K        517K

Largest executable program size          517K (528.896 bytes)
Largest free upper memory block            0K        (0 bytes)
MS-DOS is resident in the high memory area.

C:\WINDOWS>
```

Basic steps

1 Set the correct interrupt on your card - check its manual for the best setting

2 Switch off your PC, unplug the mains lead and open the case

3 Find the row of expansion connectors, remove the metal plate over the back slot of a free expansion connector

4 Press the new card firmly into the expansion connector, with the metal plate with connectors to microphone or speaker facing out

5 Secure the metal plate onto the PC's chassis using the screw you took out in step 3

6 Put the case back on, plug in the mains and switch on the PC

Installing a card

Installing a new card into your PC is one of the basic ways of expanding its functions. You might need to fit a sound card or, if you're adding a CD-ROM drive, you will need a special controller card. Cards fit inside your PC into a long connector, called an expansion connector. Most PCs have five or six connectors, but some might already be used by a graphics adapter card or hard disk controller.

The PC communicates with a card in an expansion slot using a special signal called an interrupt. Each card needs to be allocated its own interrupt number, or you'll confuse the PC. Before you install the card you need to set it to respond to an interrupt - read the manual that comes with the card to find out which is best.

Installing the driver software

When you've plugged in the new card, you still have one job to do. To allow the PC to understand how to control the card, it needs special driver software. This translates the data from the card into a form that the PC can understand. The driver software will be on a disk with your new card. Each type of software has a different installation procedure, so read your card's manual carefully and follow its instructions.

Take note

When you switch on your PC, it will carry out basic tests on itself, if there's a problem it will beep several times. Switch it off and check that you fitted the card correctly.

Setting up Windows

The last step before you can use your new card is to configure Windows and tell it about the new hardware and the driver software.

To configure Windows, use the Drivers icon in the Control Panel.

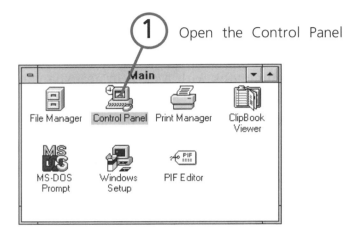

① Open the Control Panel

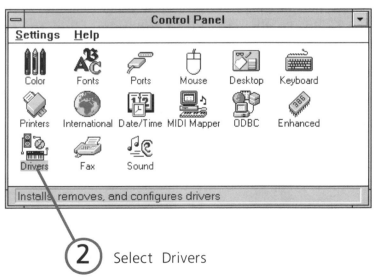

② Select Drivers

Basic steps

❏ **To configure Windows**

1 Double-click on the Control Panel icon in the Main group

2 Double-click on the Drivers icon

3 Click on the Add button

4 Insert the disk that came with your new card into drive A: , or type the drive and directory path if the file is elsewhere.

5 Highlight the driver file and click on OK

Tip

If you want to play audio CDs in your new CD-Rom drive, you will have to add the standard driver called '[MCI] CD Audio' that is supplied with Windows.

24

Take note

Some cards, such as a CD-ROM controller, do not have to be installed in Windows. The system will automatically detect that you have a new CD-ROM drive.

③ Click Add

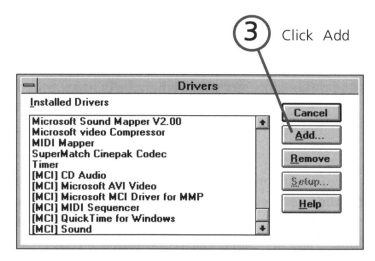

④ Insert the driver disk and click OK

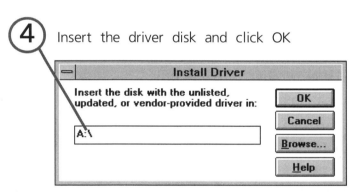

⑤ Select the driver file

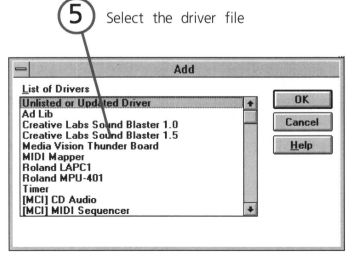

Tip

If your sound card does not work, check that the interrupt settings are correct — click on the Setup button in Step 3.

Installing more RAM

RAM (random access memory) is the high-speed memory that your PC uses to store programs and data you are using. It's much faster than disk storage, but much more expensive and will only store data when the PC is switched on. To run Windows you need at least 4Mb of RAM fitted and, for serious multimedia work, you should fit more – preferably 8Mb.

RAM is fitted in the form of electronic 'chips'. To make life easier for the user, several chips are mounted onto a tiny card called a SIMM card. Almost all PCs now take SIMM cards, since they are much easier for anyone to fit.

SIMM cards fit into SIMM sockets in your PC. These are little sockets that are around 3-4inches long. Your PC probably has four or eight sockets, and you will probably find that several are already full.

When buying more memory, you will be asked what size SIMM cards you want and what speed. Check in your PC's manual to see what type of SIMM card it requires and the speed that it supports.

1 Switch off your PC, unplug the mains lead and open the case

2 Find the row of SIMM cards fitted and the empty SIMM sockets.

3 Press the new SIMM card firmly into the expansion connector

4 Put the case back on, plug in the mains and switch on the PC

The PC detects the new memory auto-matically, but for older PCs you'll need to run the Setup utility.

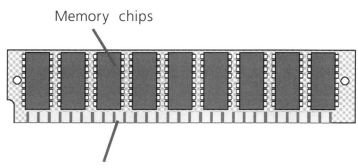

Memory chips

Gold connectors that fit into SIMM socket

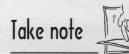

Take note

SIMM cards are very sen-sitive to static, so hold the cards by the edges and try not to touch the black squares (the RAM chips) on the cards.

Installing a CD-ROM

Fitting a CD-ROM is not very difficult, but there are several steps to the process and you must follow them carefully.

All CD-ROM drives are the same size as a 5 1/4-inch floppy disk drive. If you want to fit one into the front of your PC, you'll need to make sure that there's a free slot on your PC's fascia. Alternatively, you can use an external drive linked to your PC by a cable. The only difference is that an external drive has its own power supply.

A CD-ROM drive is controlled by a special card that fits into an expansion slot in your PC. Normally this interface between the controller card and the drive uses the SCSI standard, but some sound cards have their own interface to a CD-ROM. The newest standard is called SCSI-2 and is faster than the older SCSI standard, but will still work with older equipment.

1 Open your PC and install the controller card in a free slot – see page 23.

2 Remove the blank panel from an empty 5¼-inch drive bay in your PC's casing

3 Slide the CD-ROM drive into the bay and screw it into position

4 Connect the power cable – there should be several spare in your PC – and connect the wide, flat cable between the controller card and the drive.

5 In some drives you have the option to play music CDs through speakers: connect the two audio cables from the back of the CD-ROM drive to the sound card.

Take note

Make sure that you have the correct type of controller card for the CD-ROMdrive. If you buy an upgrade kit, everything will be compatible, otherwise try and stick to SCSI-compatible equipment as this will work together and is easier to upgrade.

Summary

- ❏ **Check what your PC has fitted** and make a list of what it needs

- ❏ Before you install a card, set the **interrupt** for the card

- ❏ To **install a card**, switch off your PC, open the case and plug in the card

- ❏ Before the card will work properly, you need to install the **driver software**

- ❏ **Installing a CD-ROM** is quite straightforward, as each cable has one – and only one – matching socket.

- ❏ If you are installing a new **CD-ROM** or more **RAM**, you don't need to configure Windows.

4 Sound

Sound Recorder

Once you have installed your sound card (see page 14) you are ready to starting recording and playing back sounds. Windows includes a utility called Sound Recorder that allows you to record a sound then save it in a standard file format called a WAV file. Once you have recorded a sound, you can use Sound Recorder to play it back, add special effects or edit it. Over the next few pages you will see how to use Sound Recorder and how to use the WAV sound file in other programs.

To start off, make sure that you have plugged in the microphone into the Mic socket of the sound card and a pair of speakers into the Speaker socket. Turn the thumb-wheel volume control on the back of the sound card to around its half-way point - you can adjust this later.

The Sound Recorder utility is stored in the Accessories group in your Windows setup. To start it, open the Accessories group and double-click on its icon. If you don't have an Accessories group, or you cannot find the Sound Recorder icon there, check with your computer manager if you work in a company (he may have removed it) or install the utility from the Windows setup disks.

Take note

The Sound Recorder uses WAV files that contain sampled sound signals. A MIDI file contains notes rather than actual sound samples.

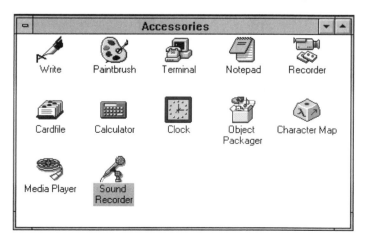

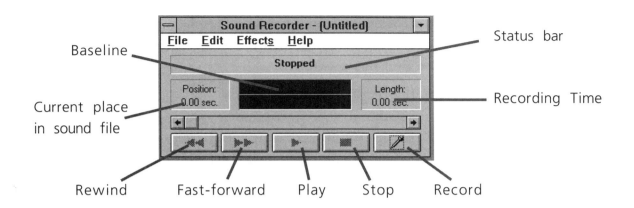

Baseline

Current place
in sound file

Status bar

Recording Time

Rewind   Fast-forward   Play   Stop   Record

When you start Sound Recorder you will see a control panel that looks very similar to a audio tape recorder. The buttons work in much the same way, allowing you to play a sound recording, rewind to the beginning, fast-forward to the end or stop during play-back.

In the central part of the panel is a thin green line running horizontally across the play-back window. This line is called the baseline. It shows the shape of the sound signal as it is being recorded or played back.

Above the baseline is the status bar that tells you what's happening: if you are recording, playing back a sound or have stopped the sound.

To the right is an indicator that tells you how long the recording is. Sound Recorder normally has a maximum recording capacity of 60 seconds - but if you record for this long the resulting file will be huge!

Tip

Try to record for no more than around 20 seconds, or the WAV file on your disk will become very big.

Recording a sound

To record a sound into digital form, use Sound Recorder. Make sure that you have the microphone plugged into the sound card and switched on (if it has a switch).

To start recording, point to the record button and click the left-hand mouse button. Speak into the microphone, but don't hold it too close to your mouth, or you will record a lot of hissing. As you speak, you'll see a waveform representation of your voice on the baseline and the current length of the recording.

Once you want to stop recording, click on the Stop button. The recorded sound is stored in memory, but it has not yet been saved permanently to disk. Use the File – Save menu option to save the sound as a WAV format file.

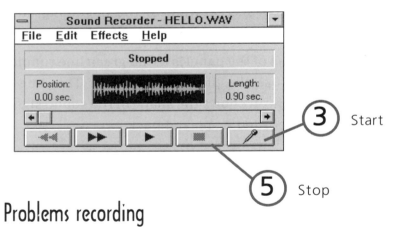

Start

Stop

Problems recording

If the baseline doesn't show a signal as you speak, make sure that you correctly selected the Record button. If you did, the status bar will display 'Recording'. If there's still no signal, you might have to set up the sound card input level. Check your card's manual to see if there is a mixer or setup utility that lets you set the input level of the microphone - some cards set it to zero by default!

1 Start Sound Recorder by double clicking on its icon

2 Hold the microphone between 8-12 inches from your mouth

3 Click on ▱ the Record button to start recording

4 Speak into the microphone

5 When you have finished, click on ■ the Stop button

6 Use **File–Save** to save your sound as a file

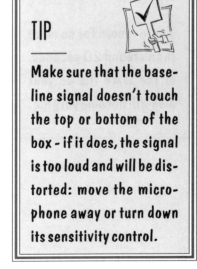

TIP

Make sure that the baseline signal doesn't touch the top or bottom of the box - if it does, the signal is too loud and will be distorted: move the microphone away or turn down its sensitivity control.

Playing back a sound

1 Select the **File–Open** menu option

2 Highlight the WAV file you saved earlier, or look in the Windows directory for samples then click **OK** to open the file

3 Click [▶] the Play button to start playing

4 Click the stop button to stop, then the rewind button to move back to the start of the sound sample

Once you have recorded and saved a sound as a WAV file you can play it back using Sound Recorder. The window title bar (in blue) will show the name of the sound file and the green baseline will show the shape of the sound wave.

To play the sound, click on the play button. The marker in the scroll bar just above the row of buttons moves to show which part of the sound is being played. To the left of the baseline is an indicator with the current position.

If you want to move to a new part of the sound file click and drag the marker in the scroll bar. To stop playing the sound, select the stop button. This doesn't move back to the start of the sound sample, so either click play again to continue or click on the fast forward or rewind buttons to move to the end or start of the sound.

Adjusting the volume

If you want to adjust the volume of the sound, you can either adjust the amplification of the sound card with its thumbwheel, or you can change the sound sample itself. To do this, see page 37 on special effects.

Tip

Click to the right of the marker on the scroll bar to move forward in the sample by one second, or to the left of the marker to move back by one second.

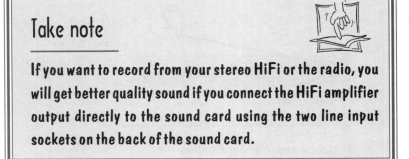

Take note

If you want to record from your stereo HiFi or the radio, you will get better quality sound if you connect the HiFi amplifier output directly to the sound card using the two line input sockets on the back of the sound card.

Editing sounds

Recording a voice or a sound does not always result in the perfect sound sample. You might pause before speaking, or cough in the middle! Sound Recorder includes simple editing functions that let you cut out sections of a sound sample that you don't want.

There are two cutting functions: one cuts any sound before the current point and the second cuts the sound after the current point. With these, you can trim a sound sample to remove, say, a cough at the start or a pause at the end. By combining them together, you can cut out sounds in the middle of your sample.

The editing functions work in relation to the current point in the sample. The point is exactly in the middle of the playback window, although since there's no line or mark, it's sometimes a little difficult to know exactly where it lies.

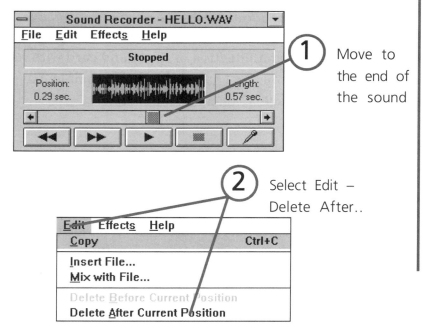

Move to the end of the sound

Select Edit – Delete After..

❏ **To cut off the end**

1 Move the marker in the scroll bar to get to the end of the sound you want. The end of the wave should be in the centre of the baseline

2 Select the **Edit – Delete After Current Position** menu option

3 A message box will ask you to confirm that you want to delete this section of the sample, click **OK** if you are sure

4 Press the Play button to check that the sample now ends at the correct point. If okay, save the file with the **File–Save** menu option. If you want to go back to the original sound, choose the **File–Revert** menu option

Running sounds together

❑ **To cut out a middle section**

1 Move to the start of the section you want to delete and delete everything after it, and save this as 'part1.wav'

2 Open your original and move to the end of the section you want to delete.

3 Delete everything before this point.

4 Move to the start of the file and use the **Edit–Insert File** command

5 Select 'part1.wav' at this point.

To add two sounds so that they run on from each other, use the Sound Recorder's **Insert File** function. This will insert an existing sound sample at the chosen point in your existing sound. For example, if you have one sound sample with you saying 'hello' and another saying 'world' you could combine them to say 'hello world'.

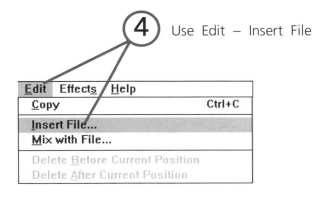

④ Use Edit – Insert File

⑤ Select the file

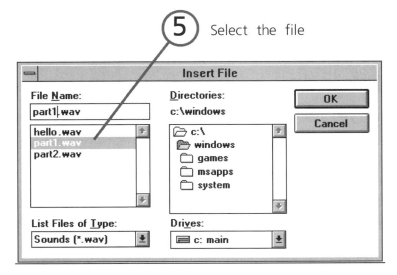

Take note

This may seem a long-winded way of doing things, but it's the only way to cut a section from the middle of a sound.

Mixing Sounds together

A good of enhancing any sound sample is to mix it with another. For example, if you want to add applause to your speech, or a background mood-music to an announcement, you need to mix two sounds together. Sound Recorder lets you combine two sound files together so that, when played, they both play simultaneously.

Record your speech or announcement and save this as one WAV file. Now record your background effects or applause and save this as a second WAV file. The Mix function in Sound Recorder will combine the two.

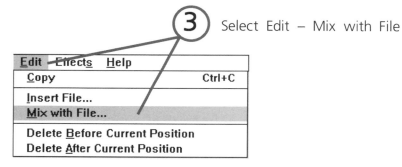

Select Edit – Mix with File

Volume levels

When you mix two sounds together, the signals are added together. This means that the overall level of the finished sound could reach the limits of your sound card and so start to distort. If your two sounds are too loud, you'll have to reduce their volume using the Edit/Reduce Volume menu option.

High volume – with distortion at the limits

Low volume – clearer signal

1 Record your speech and save it as 'sound1.wav'

2 Record your applause and save it as 'sound2.wav' – this is the file currently open

3 Select the **Edit – Mix** menu option

4 Highlight the file 'sound1.wav' and click **OK**

5 The result is a mix of sound1 and sound2. Select Play to hear your speech with applause

The Volume controls are on the **Effects** menu.

Special effects

Basic steps

❑ **To change the volume**

1 Select **File** – **Open** and highlight your sound WAV file, click **OK**

2 Choose the **Effects** – **Increase Volume** option

3 Play back the sound - it will be 25% louder

Now that you have mastered recording, editing and playing back sound samples, it's time to add some interest. Sound Recorder includes several special effects that help enhance your sounds.

● **Volume control** changes the sound wave itself, magnifying or reducing the level, and so the volume.

● Change the **speed** at which the sound is played back - you can slow down your speech or music for a casual feel.

● **Echo** gives greater depth to speech and makes it sound more natural.

● The **reverse** function that simply turns your sound around and plays it backwards!

All the effects work on the entire sound sample: you cannot choose to increase the volume of just one section.

Tip

If you double the speed of playback of a sound sample, you also shift frequency, so it sounds higher-pitched. If you double the speed of the sound playback a few times, you turn a male voice into a female or change a bass guitar into a lead guitar.

Playing audio CDs

Recording your own sounds is satisfying, but for enjoyable music while you work, use Windows' ability to play normal audio CDs. Windows' Media Player can control any MCI device, and your CD-ROM player can play either computer CD-ROMs or normal music CDs.

Before you can play back any audio CDs, you will need to install the 'MCI CD Audio driver'. Once you have done this through the Windows Control Panel, you'll see it appear as a new option under the Devices menu of the Media Player utility.

Unfortunately, the sound won't come through any speakers – unless you have a sophisticated sound card – instead, you can only hear your music through headphones plugged into the socket on the front of the CD-ROM drive.

If you don't want to listen through headphones, the only other option is to use your HiFi amplifier. Plug the computer's CD-ROM drive into the amplifier using the phono sockets on the back of the CD-ROM drive.

Basic steps

❑ **To install the driver**

1 Open the Main group, double-click on the **Control Panel** icon

2 Double-click on the **Drivers** icon

3 Scroll down the list of available drivers until you see 'MCI CD Audio' driver and select this. Click on the Add button

4 Have your Windows disks ready, in case you need to load the driver from disk

5 Close the Drivers utility. You can now use the CD-ROM to play audio discs

---

```
┌─────────────────────────────────────────┐
│ ⊟              Drivers                   │
├─────────────────────────────────────────┤
│ Installed Drivers                        │
│ ┌─────────────────────────┐  ┌────────┐  │
│ │ Microsoft Sound Mapper V2.00 ▲│ │ Close │  │
│ │ Microsoft video Compressor  │  └────────┘  │
│ │ MIDI Mapper                 │  ┌────────┐  │
│ │ SuperMatch Cinepak Codec    │  │ Add... │  │
│ │ Timer                       │  └────────┘  │
│ │ [MCI] CD Audio              │  ┌────────┐  │
│ │ [MCI] Microsoft AVI Video   │  │ Remove │  │
│ │ [MCI] Microsoft MCI Driver for MMP│ └─────┘│
│ │ [MCI] MIDI Sequencer        │  │ Setup..│  │
│ │ [MCI] QuickTime for Windows │  └────────┘  │
│ │ [MCI] Sound              ▼ │  │ Help   │  │
│ └─────────────────────────┘  └────────┘  │
└─────────────────────────────────────────┘
```

③ Select CD Audio

38

Basic steps

❏ **to play an audio disc**

1 Insert the audio CD into the drive, printed side uppermost and close the drive door

2 Open the Accessories group and double-click on the Media Player icon

3 Select the **Device** menu and choose **CD Audio** – if it's not on the list, make sure that the driver is correctly installed

4 Click on ▶ the Play button to start playing the CD

Controlling the audio CD

Media Player gives you a lot of control over how the tracks on the audio CD are played. You can change the sequence in which the tracks are played, skip through tracks, fast-forward, pause or even eject the CD.

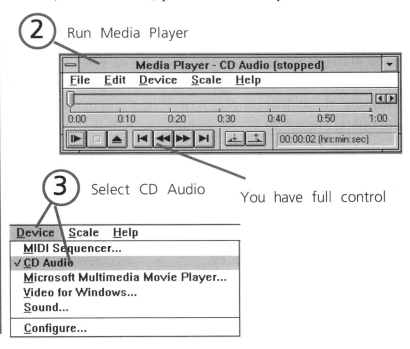

② Run Media Player

③ Select CD Audio   You have full control

Tip

If you want to listen to music while you work on a spreadsheet, load an audio disc, start Media Player, press Play then minimise the Media Player and start your spreadsheet application: the music will continue playing.

Hooking sounds

With your PC equipped with a sound card, it's hard to resist not configuring Windows to take advantage of all the new sounds that you can capture and play back. Windows has half-a-dozen sounds that it uses if there's an error (normally a bell), or a fanfare (when it starts) or scales (when you quit Windows).

Each of these actions is called a *hook*. You can assign any sound to these hooks - and there are plenty of them. For example, the bell soon gets irritating if you make a lot of mistakes; Microsoft Word sounds the bell if you try and scroll past the last line in the document. A spoken warning would be much more civilised.

The same when you start Windows - why not set it up so that your PC says 'Hello' to you and 'Goodbye' or 'thanks' when you shut down Windows? You can even get Windows to chime on the hour.

To create your own recording, use 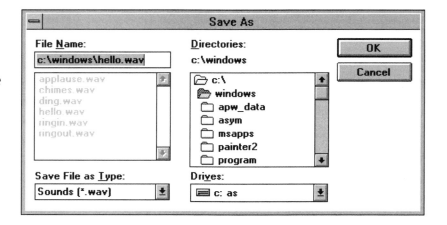 Sound Recorder (see page 32) and save the WAV file in the \Windows directory.

(see page 32)

There are a few WAV files already in Windows, to start you off. These are all assigned to hooks.

Tip

Windows includes a dozen hooks, but other applications can add their own. If you use electronic mail or other applications, you'll probably find there are more hooks.

Basic steps

1 Double-click on the Control Panel icon

2 Double-click on the Sounds icon

3 On the left is a list of the hooks or Windows events to which you can allocate a sound. Click on the Hourly Chime to highlight it.

4 On the right is a list of sound files in the \Windows directory. To assign a sound to the Hourly Chime, click on one of those listed or move to the directory where you store your sound files.

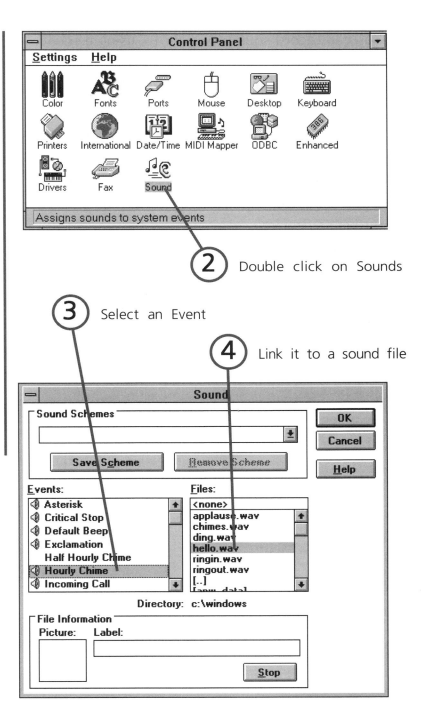

Double click on Sounds

Select an Event

Link it to a sound file

41

Summary

❑ You can **record sounds** on your PC using a sound card to convert the signal into a digital form. The Sound Recorder utility is used to record sound samples which are stored in a WAV file format.

❑ The Sound Recorder can also be used to **play back** sound samples, edit them and add special effects.

❑ The **volume** of sound samples can be adjusted either using the thumbwheel on the sound card or through software

❑ To play **audio CDs**, you need to install the correct driver then you can control your CD-ROM drive using the Media Player utility

❑ Add interest to your Windows configuration by **assigning your own sounds to events** within Windows.

5 Midi

MIDI

So far, you have experimented with WAV sound files that are digital recordings of an analogue sound wave. If you want to create more complex musical effects, or play several different instruments at the same time, you need to learn about MIDI. Unlike a WAV file, which contains the data that makes up a sound, a MIDI file contains notes. It can also contain instructions to change the instrument.

MIDI is normally used to control external electronic instruments, such as a keyboard or drum machine. However, as well as a sampler, most sound cards also have a synthesizer built into the card that can also be controlled through MIDI commands.

❏ Most sound cards have a MIDI synthesizer built in. If you have an FM synthesizer, it creates sounds by varying the frequency of a basic note – it's simple and cheap but doesn't sound as good as a waveform synthesizer: this has short recordings of 'real' instruments that are played back.

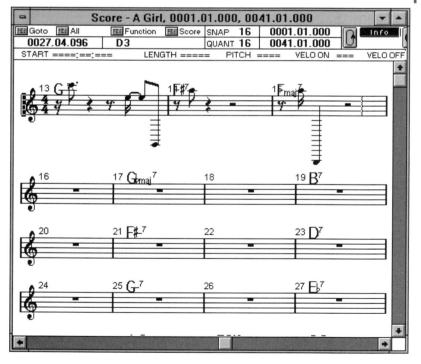

This MIDI sequencer software will record notes played on a synthesizer and display them – or you can write music directly onto the screen.

44

□ To play a tune on a MIDI synthesizer you tell it the notes to play and the instrument to use. Each instrument 'sound' is described by information called a *patch* which defines what a piano, violin or drum sound like.

If you want to control external synthesizers or a drum machine, you need to link the instruments with your PC. At the back of your sound card you'll see a 9-pin D-connector. This is the MIDI interface and it works like a high-speed serial interface (it actually transmits the data at 32.5Kbps). To control an external instrument, you will need a MIDI cable from your PC to the round connectors used by instruments: you can link several instruments together, in a daisy-chain fashion, and each can be controlled separately.

MIDI Patch Map: 'MT32'

1 based patches

Src Patch	Src Patch Name	Dest Patch	Volume %	Key Map Name
0	Acoustic Grand Piano	0	100	[None]
1	Bright Acoustic Piano	1	100	[None]
2	Electric Grand Piano	3	100	[None]
3	Honky-tonk Piano	7	100	[None]
4	Rhodes Piano	5	100	[None]
5	Chorused Piano	6	100	[None]
6	Harpsichord	17	100	[None]
7	Clavinet	21	100	[None]
8	Celesta	22	100	[None]
9	Glockenspiel	101	100	[None]
10	Music Box	101	100	[None]
11	Vibraphone	98	100	[None]
12	Marimba	104	100	[None]
13	Xylophone	103	100	[None]
14	Tubular Bells	102	100	[None]
15	Dulcimer	105	100	[None]

OK   Cancel   Help

How to use MIDI

Windows comes with several tools to use MIDI, but unfortunately include nothing that will let you compose tunes using MIDI. Your sound card may well have come with a program to let you compose notes and play them back through the synthesizer or through other instruments.

To create a tune you will need software called a sequencer. This lets you write musical notes and assign them to different instruments: remember, MIDI can play several different instruments at the same time! You can create separate tracks for each instrument and compose the notes on that track, then play the tracks back together.

The sequencer should also have a mixer to let you change the volume of each track or instrument as it is being played.

❑ As you can see, MIDI is far more flexible and powerful than a basic sound card. It takes extra software and a lot of time to understand all its functions, but it's worth while if you want to create great music.

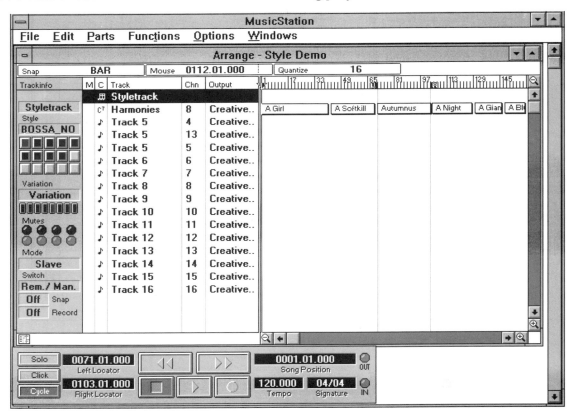

Basic steps

1 Run **Media Player**

2 Use the **File – Open** menu option to find and open your MIDI file – it will have a *mid* or *rmi* extension

3 Click ▶ the Play button

Playing MIDI

MIDI notes and instructions are stored in files with a MID extension. Once you have created a MIDI file - with a sequencer or using pre-written samples - you can play it back with the Media Player tool.

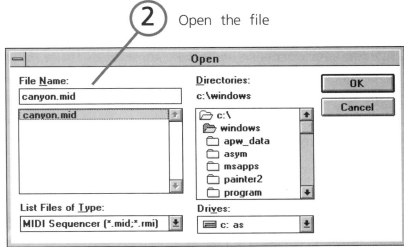

② Open the file

③ Click Play

Music Station

This is a MIDI sequencer program that lets you record MIDI notes, edit them and play them back through different instrument patches. (Opposite)

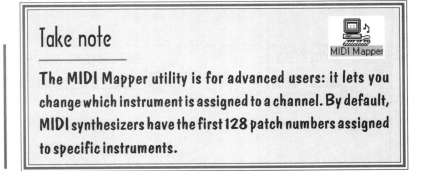

Take note

The MIDI Mapper utility is for advanced users: it lets you change which instrument is assigned to a channel. By default, MIDI synthesizers have the first 128 patch numbers assigned to specific instruments.

Connecting MIDI devices

If you have an external electronic instrument with a MIDI interface, you can plug it into the MIDI port on your sound card and control it from the sequencer.

You will need to buy a MIDI cable for your sound card. This plugs into the connector on the back of the card and feeds into two leads with round connectors. External instruments normally have two, sometimes three, MIDI sockets. These are labeled 'in', 'out' and 'thru'. You can connect up to 32 instruments together in a daisy-chain fashion and control them all from the sequencer software that's running on your PC.

Plug the cable from your PC into the 'in' socket of the first instrument, then a second cable from this from the 'thru' socket to the 'in' socket of the second instrument. This should lead back to the second MIDI lead on your PC.

Recording from MIDI

You can use your PC not only as a sequencer, but also as a recorder to record the notes played on other MIDI instruments. For example, if you can play the piano, you could set up your sequencer to record the notes generated by the electronic piano. Once you have recorded the notes you can play them back through any other instrument!

Take note

Can't write music? If you cannot read or write music, don't worry. Most sequencer software lets you create notes using symbols. It can also correct timing faults and generally turn your music into a professional-sounding composition.

The control panel of many MIDI sequencers will display the speed at which you are playing notes and it is recording, and you can make a 'click' to help you keep time.

Advanced MIDI Software

❑ MIDI sequencer software can look daunting, but it's straightforward to use. There is normally an area where you can write the musical notes, and a mixing desk to vary the volume of the different instruments in the final work.

MIDI is the standard that's used by thousands of professional musicians. With a computer, you can have as much power as a professional recording studio sitting on your desk.

If you want to compose your own music using MIDI, you will have to buy special MIDI sequencer software. This lets you compose music for several instruments at a time, and then mix their sounds together to create the finished work.

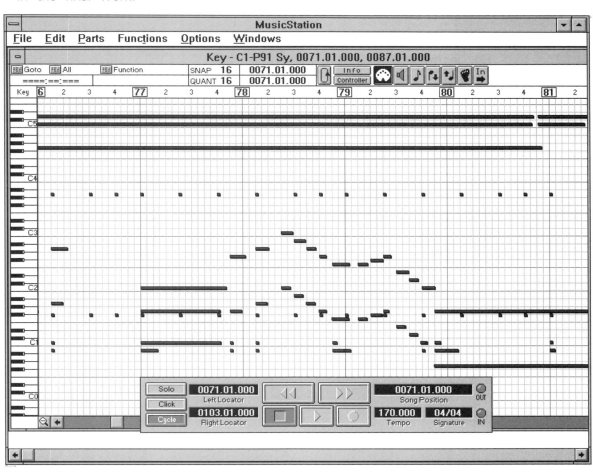

Summary

❑ MIDI is a high-speed serial link that can connect your PC to **external electronic instruments**

❑ MIDI stores **notes and commands** to control instruments, rather than sound waves

❑ Windows comes with software to play back files with MIDI notes, but you need **sequencer software** to create your own tunes

❑ MIDI allows you to play many **different instruments** at the same time – to create your own orchestra!

❑ MIDI is the most flexible and powerful method of producing **musical effects**

❑ The **first 128 instrument sounds** in a synthesizer are usually always the same – until you change them! This means that if you want to use an oboe, you select channel 68

6 Images and graphics

Graphics

The way to make any multimedia presentation really stand out is with sparkling graphics. Windows includes a paint program, Paintbrush, that lets you create simple, effective images. It's not really suitable for anything too complex, but for backgrounds, titles or simple animation it's good enough. Lastly, if you have a hand-scanner, you can use Paintbrush to edit the images scanned, add special effects or crop the picture to the size you want.

Paintbrush can read and save bitmap graphic images in two of the most popular file formats: BMP and PCX. You can import images created with Paintbrush into just about any authoring program, presentation software or even your Windows wordprocessor application.

Whichever type of graphics program you use, you should know about the different file formats. The most popular are TIFF, BMP and PCX. Each of these stores black and white or colour images in a slightly different way.

Take note

With vector graphics, if you change their scale they will always look the same and be of the same quality. If you zoom in on a bitmap graphic image, you'll magnify all the individual pixels and it will lose its definition.

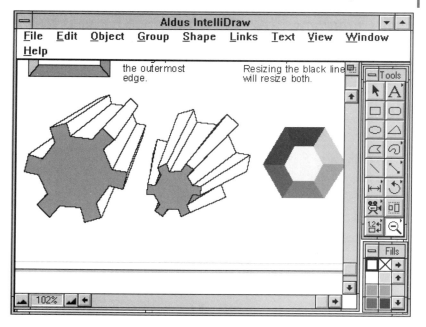

A vector graphic in Aldus IntelliDraw. The shapes are drawn with line 'vectors' and these remain as sharp even if you zoom in close.

File formats

The most important difference is in the type of image you are drawing. There are two types:

- **Vector graphics** describe a shape or image using lines and curves and the image is stored as a series of co-ordinates.

- **Bitmap images** are made up of pixels, tiny dots on your screen or printer, each of which you can paint a particular colour.

Below, a bitmapped graphic in Paintbrush. Later on, you'll see how to edit the image and add more towers to the castle!

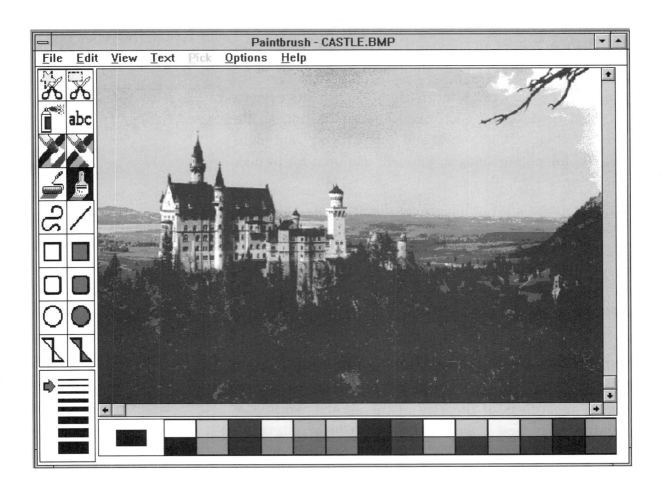

Colours

Each pixel in a colour bitmap images can be painted a different colour. You'll often see paint programs described with the number of colours they can use. Windows' Paintbrush can only paint in 28 different colours, but you can choose the 28 colours from a larger palette with millions of colours.

To understand colours, you need to understand how colours are stored in a computer. In a black and white display, each pixel can be either on or off: so uses one bit of data. If you assign two bits of data to each pixel, it can be one of four possible colours. With eight bits, it can display one of 256 colours and for 24-bit colour each pixel can display one of 16.7million colours. (See page 11 on graphics adapters for more details.)

The more colours you want to use, the more bits have to be used to describe each pixel and so the image file becomes bigger. Like sound and video, if you want high-quality, full-colour images, you will use up a lot of disk space since each file can easily grow to 2Mb.

When you use a lot of images in a multimedia book, the book soon starts to grow in size, too. That's one of the reasons why so many colourful multimedia titles are sold on CD-ROM - nothing else can store as much data.

Resolution

As well as different colours, images are displayed in different resolutions (the number of pixels in each unit area). A VGA monitor has a maximum resolution of 640x480 pixels, regardless of the size of the screen. An S-VGA monitor goes better with either 800x600 or 1024x768 pixels, and so images look sharper and better defined.

Take note

Any computer image is better than a television, which has surprisingly poor quality - but because of the movement, your eyes don't notice the resolution (until you press freeze-frame on your video player).

Paintbrush tools

Paintbrush

❏ **To define a colour**

1 Double click with the right mouse button on the palette colour you want to change

A panel with three sliders appear. These define the amount of red, green and blue in the colour

2 Drag the sliders to change the colour.

3 Click **OK** when you're happy with the colour

To start using Paintbrush, open the Accessories group and double-click on its icon. Running down the left of the screen are two columns of tools, along the bottom of the screen is the palette of available colours. The main blank area of the screen is your canvas.

To draw freehand, select the brush tool, then move to the palette and click once with the left button to choose the ink, (click with the right button to define the colour of the background). Lastly, click on the lines in the bottom left corner to choose the width of the brush.

If you are using clip art or scanned images, they may need to be re-sized. You can set the size of the canvas (with the **Options – Image Attributes** command), but you cannot resize an existing image in Paintbrush: to do this you need a more sophisticated paint program. (See page 60)

Choosing a palette

Paintbrush can use a limited palette of 28 colours for any image, but you can define each of these 16 colours from a source of over 16million possible colours.

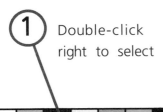

① Double-click right to select

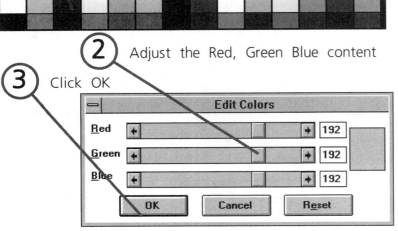

② Adjust the Red, Green Blue content

③ Click OK

Edit Colors

Red	← ▮ →	192
Green	← ▮ →	192
Blue	← ▮ →	192

OK Cancel Reset

Take note

For more colours, or more sophisticated palette control, you need paint software that's more advanced than Paintbrush. (See page 60)

Editing images

You will probably find Paintbrush most useful to retouch or edit existing images that you have scanned in or taken from a clip-art source. Paintbrush includes tools to duplicate an area, delete sections and paint one pixel at a time.

When your image has one rose, why not create a bunch of roses? If a background has one mountain, give it three. You can do this invisibly by using the copy and paste commands of Paintbrush. First, define the area you want to copy, copy it to the Clipboard (an area of memory that can temporarily store images, sound or text) and paste it in where you want.

Basic steps

❑ **To duplicate part of an image**

1 Open the image file using **File—Open** — remember, Paintbrush only reads PCX or BMP files

2 Click on the freehand scissor tool in the top right of the toolbar

Cutting tools

Air brush

Text

Erasers

Fill

Brush

Lines

Shapes

Line width

3 Move the pointer to one edge of the image to be duplicated, hold down the right button and trace around it

4 When you've finished, release the right mouse button

5 Select the **Edit–Copy** command to copy the section of the image to the Clipboard

6 Select the **Edit–Paste** command and you'll see a duplicate image appear at the top left

7 Drag the new image into position

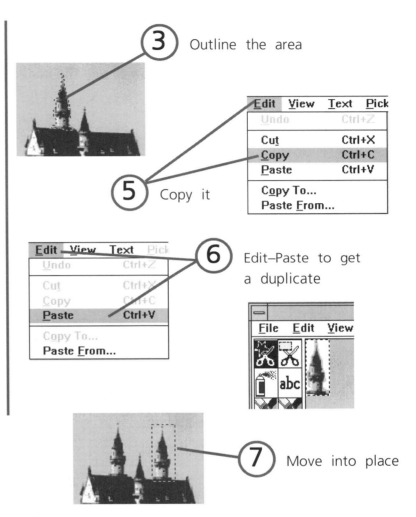

(3) Outline the area

(5) Copy it

(6) Edit–Paste to get a duplicate

(7) Move into place

Take note

You can copy part of an image from one picture to another. Follow steps 1-5 to get the copy from the first picture, then open the second file and paste the image into it.

Moving images

To move an object around an image, use the same technique: once you have defined the shape you want to move, with the freehand scissor tool, click and drag it to its new position. You don't have to cut or paste it.

Retouching images

Often when you scan in an image, you may need to edit it to get rid of a background that's distracting or little speckles that ruin the image, here's how to edit the image at a fine, pixel-by-pixel level.

Basic steps

1 Select the **View–Zoom In** menu option

2 Move the selection box to the area you want to edit, and click on the right button to get a magnified view

3 Select colours from the palette for the ink (left button) and the background (right button)

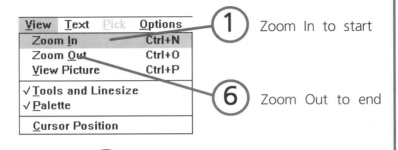

(1) Zoom In to start

(6) Zoom Out to end

(4) Click to change colour

(3) Select colours

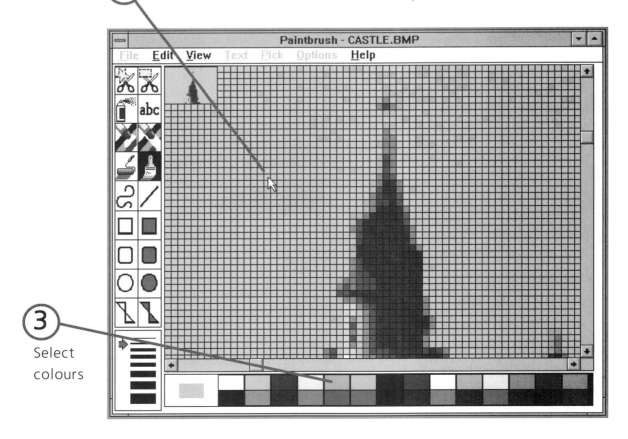

58

4 Move to the pixel you want to edit and click once with the left button to set it to the ink colour and once with the right button to set it to the background colour

5 Repeat as necessary, using the scroll bars to move over the image

6 Select the **View–Zoom Out** menu option to see the whole image

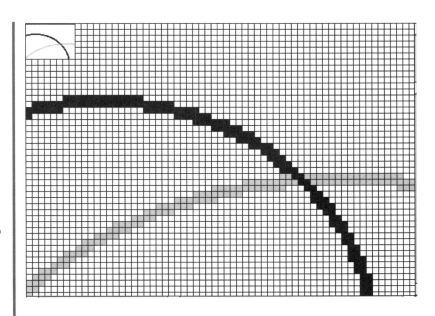

Dots of a lighter shade will smooth a jagged line

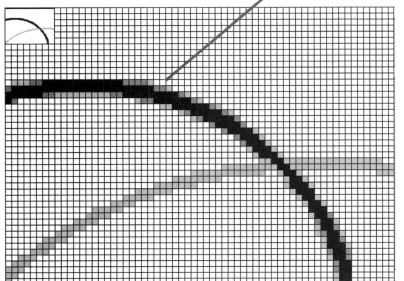

Tip

If you want to smooth out a line or curve so that it appears less jagged, add a lighter shade of the colour in the 'jags' and your eye will make it smoother.

Other graphics programs

There are two big advantages of Paintbrush: first, it's free and second it's easy to use. Unfortunately, if you want to create complex graphics or special effects, then it soon shows its limitations. Multimedia applications use a lot of graphics in different ways and if you want to explore further you should really consider buying more advanced graphics software.

When editing full-colour photographic-quality images on-screen you really need special software designed to do the job. To design complex three-dimensional models, accurate graphics or landscapes you need different software. If you need to create icons or special pointers, you'll need different graphics software again.

Many authoring packages include drawing utilities. 'Asymetrix' ToolBook includes an icon and cursor editor that lets you design your own icons and cursor shapes to use in your application.

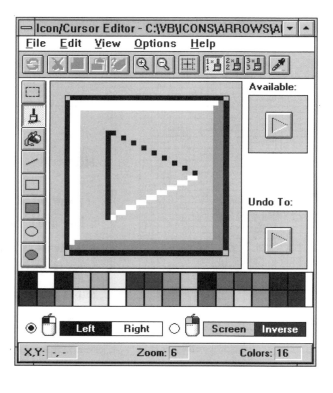

Publisher's Paintbrush is similar to Windows' Paintbrush but provides better palette control (see the bottom of the screen) and more complex editing tools. One of these, shown in the foreground, lets you adjust the brightness and contrast of the image.

These pages show you some of the tools available to a multimedia designer. Like any graphics software, they won't help your creative skills or turn you into an artist - but they won't impose restrictions and will let you draw anything you want.

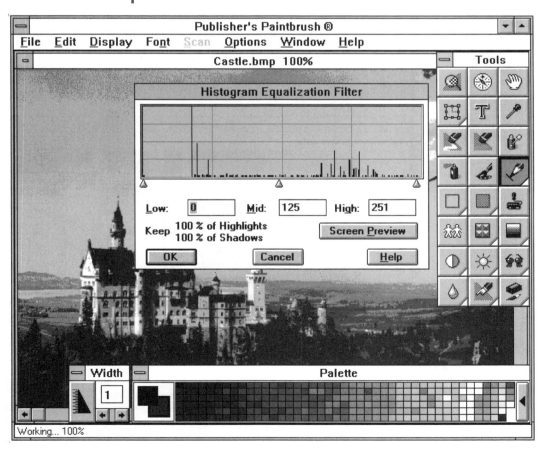

Photo editing software

Paintbrush can display 28 colours to use in an image - but this is very limiting when editing photographic-quality images. More advanced programs, such as Photoshop give you access to over 16.7million colours from a colour-wheel on screen.

Advanced photo editing programs also include an 'electronic darkroom' that lets you change the contrast of parts of an image, sharpen the image or apply special filters - such as diffuser.

❑ With a powerful photo editing program you have as much control over the finished image as a photographer in a darkroom; you can darken or lighten areas, sharpen or diffuse shapes and change tones and colours.

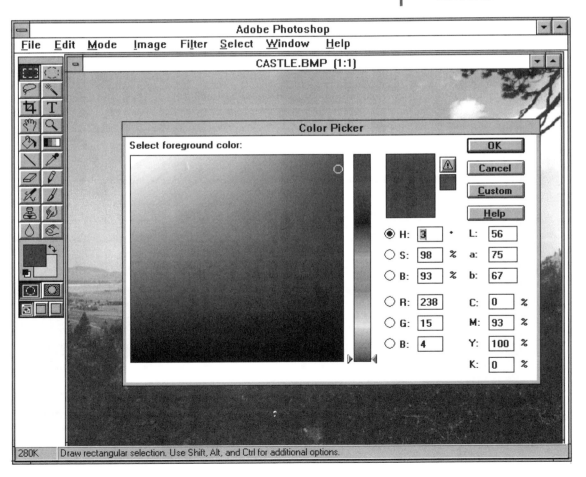

The Levels function of Photoshop displays the intensity and distribution of colours in an image.

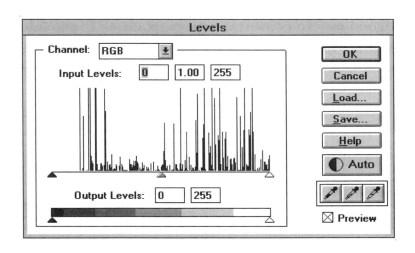

Paint Software

Paint software is now very advanced with products like Painter. This simulates different types of drawing tools - pen, brush, chalk, crayon - and also different types of paper. You can draw with a pressure sensitive tablet and the medium acts just like the real thing.

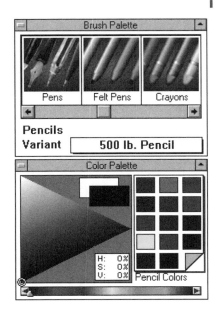

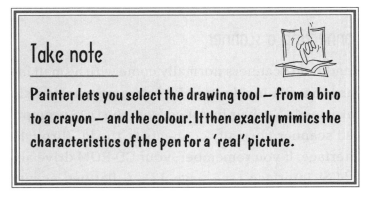

Take note

Painter lets you select the drawing tool — from a biro to a crayon — and the colour. It then exactly mimics the characteristics of the pen for a 'real' picture.

Using a Scanner

A good way to convert drawings, plans or a logo into a graphics file is to use a scanner. There are many different types of scanner. The main two types are hand-held and flat-bed scanners. Hand-held scanners look rather like a fat mouse, and are dragged over the picture to capture the image. Flat-bed scanners sit on your desk and look rather like a small photocopier.

Both types of scanner work in basically the same way: a beam of light is shone onto the original image and a photo-electric detector picks up the reflection and measures its intensity. This reading represents one pixel; the beam of light passes over the entire piece of paper to convert it into a bitmap graphic file.

A flat-bed scanner is more accurate, and more expensive than a hand-held scanner since it uses a motorised beam of light rather than relying on you to drag it over the paper. Both types of scanner can detect black and white, grey-scale or colour images in different resolutions.

The normal type of scanner can detect 300 dots per inch (similar to the output of a laser printer) with eight-bit colour or grey-scale to give 256 different levels.

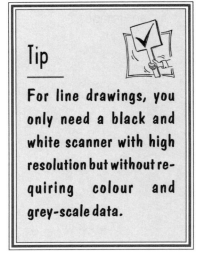

Tip

For line drawings, you only need a black and white scanner with high resolution but without requiring colour and grey-scale data.

Connecting a scanner

Hand-held scanners normally come with a small interface card that fits inside your PC into an expansion slot. The card needs a driver installed from the DOS prompt. A flat-bed scanner normally connects to the PC through a SCSI interface. If you remember, your CD-ROM drive also uses a SCSI interface (see page 12). A flat-bed scanner can simply plug into the existing controller (or the back of the CD-ROM drive) and it should work correctly.

Basic steps

❏ **To tilt an image**

1 Run Paintbrush and open the file containing the image.

2 Select the square scissor tool and stretch a box around the section of the image that you want to tilt

3 Choose the **Pick–Tilt** menu option. Your pointer turns into a crosshair.

4 Move the pointer to the outline box and drag the box until it tilts to the angle that you want

Controlling a scanner

Many types of paint and photo-retouching software packages include support for scanners. Some DTP programs, such as Corel Ventura, also include support for a scanner. The software detects if there's a scanner installed and add a new menu item to the menu bar.

Using scanned images

Once you have scanned a picture, the scanner software will let you crop the scan to the correct size then save it as a graphics file: this could be as a TIFF, PCX or BMP file. If you want to retouch or edit the image, you could open the file in a paint program. You can then use the image in any multimedia authoring program or import it into your wordprocessor or database.

Tilting an image

When scanning, it's often difficult to get the original image exactly square - especially if you're using a hand-held scanner. The same problems happen when you take a photograph and then want to use the image from the PhotoCD (see page 66). Paintbrush includes a function that will tilt any area of an image. It is not as good as the rotate function seen in many advanced programs, but it will sort out a lot of problems.

Using PhotoCD

One of the most exciting new ways of capturing images to use in your multimedia programs is called Kodak PhotoCD. It's really very simple: use your normal camera to take photographs on normal film then, when you take the film to the chemist to be developed, ask them to produce a PhotoCD at the same time. You'll get your prints back together with a CD-ROM and this won't cost too much extra. The CD-ROM contains very high-resolution scans of your photographs in millions of colours that you can then use in any paint program.

To read the PhotoCD you have to make sure that your CD-ROM drive is PhotoCD compatible (it should say that it is CD-XA, multisession or PhotoCD compatible).

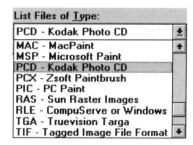

The PhotoCD includes several scans of each photograph at different resolutions and stored in various formats. This lets you test out your special effects on the smaller, low resolution images, which can be processed quickly.

1 Take your photographs with a camera and colour film as normal

2 Take the film to a Kodak chemist and ask for a PhotoCD as well as your prints

3 This takes a little longer and costs more

4 Then you get your CD-ROM, insert it into your drive

5 Use PhotoCD access software or a graphics program to open one of the files on the disc

❑ Once you have your photographs on PhotoCD, you can edit the images or use them in any presentation. Make sure that your graphics or paint software can read the TIFF or PCD format in which the images are stored.

Clip-art

A good alternative if you don't have a scanner or camera is to use ready-made clip-art. There are thousands of libraries of art work and photographs that you can buy or rent to use in a presentation, multimedia application or book. If you have a presentation graphics program, you'll find it has hundreds of symbols and pre-drawn artwork that you can use, modify and include in your work – from stars, flags and computers, to cars and people.

Many photographers now supply libraries of their work on disc and you can either buy the disc or buy the right to use one image for a particular project. Look in CD-ROM catalogues for clip-art and photographic libraries that you can use: but make sure that you read the copyright and fee scheme first.

Different graphics software handles clip-art in different ways. For example, the presentation software Harvard Graphics has a library of images that are in a special format, and can only be accessed through Harvard. You see a list of tiny representations of the images, and can paste it into your picture. Other programs supply standard clip-art in TIFF or PCX file formats.

Tip

If you draw your own work, start to keep copies of the originals which you can then use at a later date and so create your own clip-art library.

Tip

Paint Shop Pro can handle many different graphics formats, and convert from one format to another, as well as offering a full range of editing facilities — and it's shareware!

Summary

❑ You can **create your own colour images** with Paintbrush in the Accessories group of Windows

❑ **Paintbrush** includes basic tools to edit your image, re-touch detail or change colours

❑ With the Scissor tool and the **Edit–Copy/Paste** commands, you can duplicate areas of your image

❑ **Advanced graphics applications** turn your PC into an electronic darkroom and give you control over the con-trast, colour and effects

❑ To convert a picture, drawing or logo from paper to an image file use a **scanner**

❑ **Hand-held scanners** are cheap, but can distort an image unless you have a steady hand.

❑ **Flat-bed scanners** connect to the same SCSI port that controls your CD-ROM, are more accurate but more expensive than a hand-held.

❑ If you have a camera, use the cheap **PhotoCD** service to convert your film into colour graphic images on a CD-ROM.

❑ If you cannot draw, are stuck for ideas or time, use a **clip-art** library that has hundreds of pre-drawn symbols, maps, flags, and people that can be imported into your graphics program.

7 Video and Animation

Video

The ultimate in multimedia is to use video clips. This is more complicated than any other multimedia technology and you need a lot of expensive equipment to record video clips. The good news is that once you have recorded a video clip, anyone can play it back without needing any special equipment.

A video clip is made up of a series of separate frames, each one is a single colour image and is slightly different from the last. When the frames are played back fast enough, your eye sees them as continuous motion. To display smooth video, you need to show between 15 and 25 frames every second. Any less than this and the movements won't be smooth.

The frames in a video clip are colour bitmap images, so you can imagine that even a few seconds of video will take up a huge amount of disk space (ten seconds of video is equivalent to 150 frames, or 150 single image files). To cut down the space required, there are several different ways of storing the frames in a compressed format. The most popular method in Windows is called *AVI* (Audio Video Interleaved), although there is also the Apple Macintosh *QuickTime* format that runs on a Macintosh or PC.

An AVI video clip can be played by Media Player or any other video editing software. This panel shows the control over video, sound and position in the sequence.

Any video sequence is made up of a series of separate images, each sllightly different.

How it works

- The video card works a bit like a very high-speed sound card. When recording, it grabs each frame of video and converts this to a bitmap, then stores this on disk as one of a sequence.

- Once you have re-corded the video signals as a series of bitmap frames, these are compressed and stored as an AVI file. AVI video files can also store sound, which is converted into a digital form in the same way that your sound card works.

- Video capture cards can be used to either record a video clip or to grab a single frame - this is another source of still images to use in your multimedia experiments.

Recording Video

In order to record video onto your PC you will need a video capture card. This fits into an expansion slot inside your PC and connects either to a normal video camera or a VCR.

With a video card installed, you can watch the pictures it's receiving. This works through a combination of software and hardware. The software displays an empty window on the screen and colours it a special colour (called the chroma key). The video card instructs your graphics adapter to display the video images anywhere where the special colour is being displayed.

Video Playback

One of the decisions you have to make when playing back a video file is what compromise do you want to make between the size of the playback window and the quality of the video. Windows is not perfect, and cannot play back a recorded television-quality video clip that fills the screen. In practice, if you want a sharp, clear image you will have to limit the play back window to around just a few inches square.

The reason is because Windows is not fast enough to de-compress the compressed images that make up each frame at the high resolution you need to fill the entire screen. The size of the play back window is actually determined by the speed of your PC, video card and hard disk. Windows will work this out and try and display the optimum: best picture quality at the largest window size possible.

The Ultimate Video System

The way to get the best quality video recording and full-screen video play back is to fit a special card. Not only will the card compress each frame in the sequence but it will work the other way around and de-compress the frames. Because there is a special processor on this card, it works much faster than Windows on your PC so you view the video in a bigger play back window and a see better quality image. The problem is the price.

The Practical Video System

As an alternative to using the video compression card described above, Microsoft developed Video for Windows. You still need a video capture card, but then a set of programs lets you compress a video clip and de-compress during play back through software, without requiring a special compression card. It's not quite as sophisticated as the compression card described above, and the video files take up more space on disk, but it's a lot cheaper. In fact, the software to playback video clips using Video for Windows is included free with most multimedia applications and Windows itself: the Media Player utility can play back AVI format files.

Video for Windows stores the video frames in a file format called AVI. Once you have recorded a video clip as a standard AVI file, you can play it back within a playback window or include it in your multimedia presentation. Windows can treat a video clip like a sound file or image and embed it within another document (see page 103 for further details).

> **Take note**
>
> The way AVI and many other video formats store video is to only store the differences between each frame and the previous. This means that for most sequences, the size of the video file is kept smaller and the processing time is reduced.

Using Media Player

❏ **To play a video clip**

1 Double-click on the Media Player icon

2 Select **File–Open** and highlight the AVI file you want to open

The display now shows a playback window with the first frame displayed, the Media Player window is still displayed and now shows the length of the video clip and play control buttons

3 Click on ▶ and the video clip will play (with sound)

The most usual way of playing a video clip is to use the Media Player utility that's in the Accessories group. You have probably already used this flexible tool to play MIDI or sound files. It also plays back AVI-format video clips without any special hardware.

② Select an AVI file

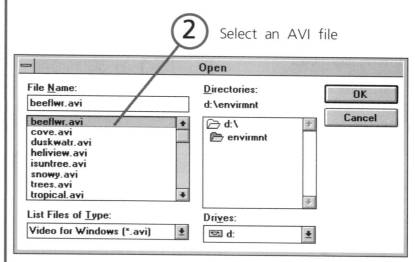

③ Click to play

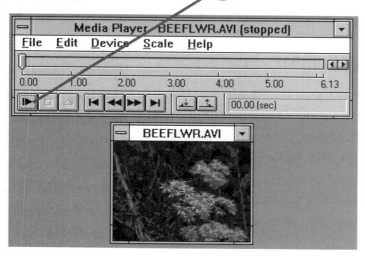

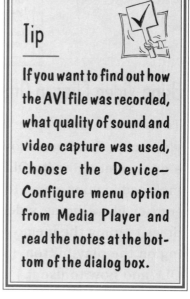

Tip

If you want to find out how the AVI file was recorded, what quality of sound and video capture was used, choose the Device–Configure menu option from Media Player and read the notes at the bottom of the dialog box.

Configure Playback

Media Player lets you configure some of the ways in which the video clip is displayed and played back. For example, if you are not concerned about the definition or quality of the video clip, but want a larger image, you can set Media Player to play back filling the whole screen rather than the small default window.

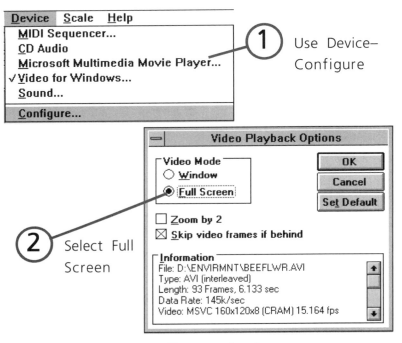

① Use Device–Configure

② Select Full Screen

Using Video Clips in Other Applications

To liven up a dull report or memo, you could add a short video clip! Windows allows you to insert an AVI file into a document using its OLE technology. The video clip in included in your memo together with basic play controls (rather like a home video recorder). Anyone with Windows reading the memo can play the video clip by clicking on the play button. (See page 99 for more details on OLE and how to use it.)

(See page 99 for more details on OLE and how to use it.)

Basic steps

1 Select the Device–Configure command

2 In the dialog box, select the **Full Screen** option and click **OK**

3 Press the play button. The image will be bigger, but the pixels will also be much bigger.

Although called full-screen, often the video doesn't fill the entire screen, but has a black border around it – this is normal

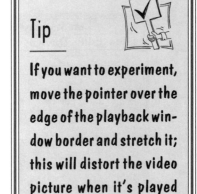

Tip

If you want to experiment, move the pointer over the edge of the playback window border and stretch it; this will distort the video picture when it's played back and produce interesting effects.

Record your own video

Basic steps

❑ **To set up to record video**

1 Install the video capture card in your PC

2 Plug a camera or VCR into the capture card

3 Plug a microphone into the capture card

4 Install the software

Take note

To record your own video clips, you will need to buy and install a lot of extra, expensive equipment.

At the start of this chapter, you found out that you need a video capture card in order to record video onto your PC's hard disk. Each frame of a video sequence is only displayed for 1/30th of a second before it is replaced with the next, so the capture card has to work fast. It stores the video image onto your hard disk in sequence, and also records any sound at the same time so that the sound is synchronised correctly with the action.

You also need a video camera or VCR with a tape of the action you want to record.

The video capture software will display whatever's 'seen' by the camera in a window on your screen. When you want to record a video clip, select the record button. Most capture cards will also let you capture a single frame (a grab) to use as a still image.

Once you have recorded the video sequence as an AVI file, it can be played back using the Media Player utility (in the Accessories group) or can be inserted into a presentation.

Editing Video

Once you have the raw footage recorded onto your PC you can edit it to change the frame sequence, cut out unwanted sections or re-record the sound. With the right software, a PC can be a professional video editing suite.

All the video editors work on the same principles. If you are editing professional video sequences, you will need to understand SMPTE which is a way of identifying each frame in a sequence. It's rather simpler for non-professional editing since each frame is normally numbered.

In order to cut out a frame, or create a new sequence, you enter an EDL (edit definition list). This tells the software what changes to make, for example 'delete frame 44'. The edit software will then re-build the video file looking at the EDL and making all the changes. Professional video editors work in a similar way, creating an EDL, but this is then passed to an automatic video recorder that creates a new video tape rather than a file on a PC.

Take note

If you have a video capture card, it will include editing software. Alternatively, products such as Microsoft's Video for Windows have editing functions and some authoring systems, such as Asymetrix Toolbook include a video editor.

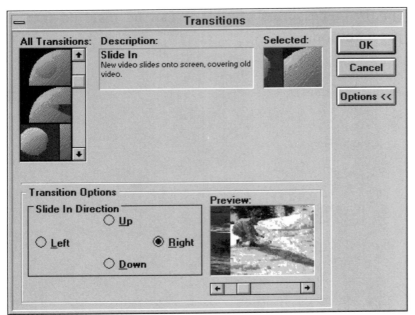

Defining a transition between two video clips, using the editor included with the Toolbook authoring software. (See Special Effects, opposite)

Video Special Effects

□ Video editor software also lets you create *mattes*. A matte uses two different sections of video that are blended with one video clip replacing one colour in the other clip. It's a very useful technique to create the illusion of flying or for similar effects.

To do this, record the first clip of someone against a plain blue background.

Now record a second clip of a moving scene or sky. The video editor software will replace the plain blue background of the first clip with the second, giving a combined effect.

The editing software normally lets you load two video clips at the same time. You can then mix these, create special effects so that one will gradually fade as the second clip appears, or cut frames from one and insert them in the other.

● A *wipe* effect is like drawing a curtain to reveal the second video under the first. It's useful for titles.

● A *dissolve* effect gradually makes the first video clip lighter while the second appears through the first.

Video editing software will also allow you to define new colours (termed the palette) for your final result and, if you need to save space, you can compress the video file.

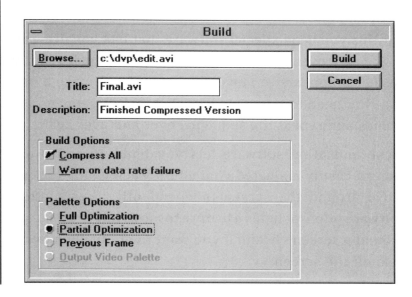

Setting the compression options before building the final version of the edited video clip.

Animation software

Video clips are not the only way to add movement and action to your multimedia presentation. A far simpler method is to use animation. It's similar to video in that a sequence of separate still images (each called a frame) is displayed rapidly in sequence and gives the impression of movement. Animation is great for moving a logo across a presentation, adding fun to an icon or to explain how something works.

A sequence of animation frames are stored in a file. There are several different file formats in which the frames can be stored, either with a FLI filename extension, FLC or AVI (like the video clips described earlier).

Create an animation

For this you need special software that lets you draw an image and, over several frames, change part of it slightly so that it appears to move. For example, to make a dog run, you need to move his legs slightly in a sequence of frames and repeat the sequence over and over again.

Some animation software lets you build an animation using a cast of animated characters. Each character can move around the screen independently. Presentation software often includes a feature to move text or an image around a screen - useful if you want to gradually move a logo off the screen.

Some sophisticated animation software includes a *tweening* function. This lets you draw the starting position of an image and the end position, and the software will work out the steps and changes required to move from the first to the last, saving you a lot of time.

Tip

For smooth animation, a sequences needs to run at the same speed as a video clip: around 30 frames per second. However, simple animation can run at 10 frames per second. As the images are often simpler, shorter and smaller than a video clip, animation files are normally much smaller.

Animation techniques

Animations are much simpler to create than you might think. And they need much less disk space and expensive equipment than video.

An animation sequence normally has a very simple or static background. This is called a *cel*. On top of the cel you place a character or actor, which can be moved according to your instructions.

The actor might have a sequence of repeated movements, perhaps to move his legs to give the impression of walking. If the actor is moved around the cel, he'll look as if he's walking on the same spot.

Take note

There are two types of animation. Path animation moves an unchanging object around the screen. Cel-based is much more powerful and lets you display a sequence of slightly different cels to give the impression of movement.

Setting the movement path for a simple object

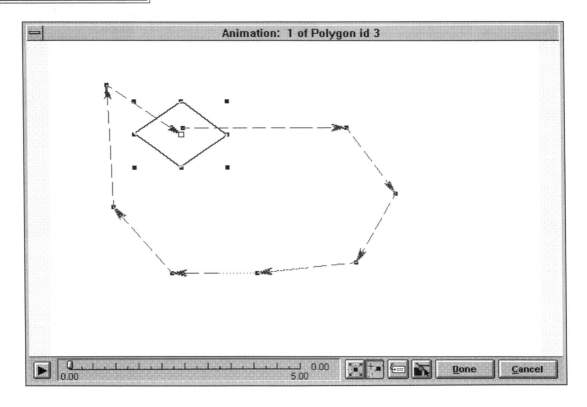

Morphing Software

Another technique that's similar to animation is called morphing. This is rather like tweening, in that you define the start image and the end image, but the two images are normally completely different. The software then works out a sequence of steps so that the first image appears to change gradually into the second object.

It's a very effective technique if used sparingly in a multimedia title: perhaps to change a computer into a wolf!

Tip

There are many software packages available, including shareware that you can try for free - like WinImages Morph.

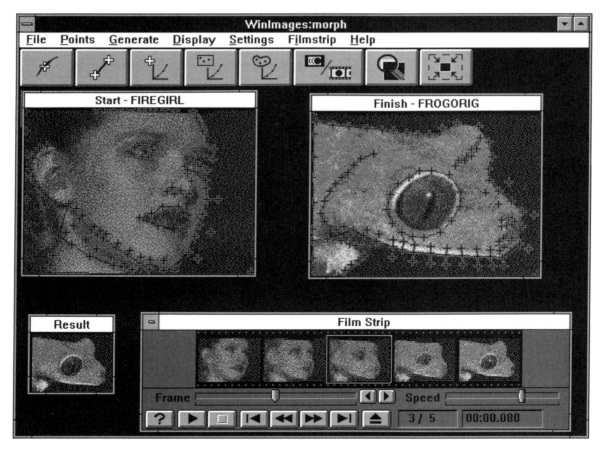

How it works

To change the girl (in the left-hand frame) into the frog (in the right-hand frame), you can specify the number of frames you want the animation sequence to span and the resolution of the final sequence.

The program works using points of reference. If you look carefully at each image, you'll see the points I have marked around the girl's and frog's heads that should be used to change the shape of the first image.

Finally, the program calculates how to change the position of the points marked and generates each frame of the finished animation.

The more frames you have, the smoother the animation.

Sequence Controls

Frame Control

Total Frames: `5`

Begin Frame #: `1`

Finish Frame #: `5`

Current Frame #: `4`

OK

Cancel

☒ Use Anti - aliasing method

☒ Save Result

Output File

`C:\IMAGES\girlfrog` . `FLC`

Output Image Path+Name   Extension

Specify

Output Size

`96` x `72`

Horizontal   Vertical

Match Start Aspect Ratio

Match End Aspect Ratio

Set to Start Frame Size

Set to End Frame Size

The Apect Ratio is the proportion of width to height. This may be different in the start and end frames. You can make the in-between frames to match either, or set a specific size.

Summary

❑ You can record video clips onto your hard disk by fitting a **video capture card** and connecting it to a video camera or VCR. Sound is recorded at the same time as movement

❑ The video clips are made up of a **sequence of images**, rapidly displayed to give the impression of movement.

❑ Video clips are normally stored in the **AVI file format**. These can be played back on any PC and do not need special hardware

❑ The **Media Player** utility in the Accessories group is used to open and play an AVI file

❑ **Video editing** software normally comes with a video capture card or can be bought separately. It allows you to cut frames, change the sequence or add special effects

❑ **Animation software** lets you create simpler animation sequences that can be very effective

❑ **Morphing** automatically animates the change of one image into another as a special effect

8 Using a CD-ROM

Accessing a CD-ROM

Once you have plugged in the controller card, connected it to your CD-ROM drive and installed the software correctly (see Chapter 2), you're ready to access CD-ROMs.

The CD-ROM drive will normally appear as drive D: under DOS and Windows. If you have two hard disk drives, or are connected to a network, it might be called a different letter, but it will work in the same way.

Open the drive bay by pressing the eject button on the front of the drive. Place the CD-ROM, printed side up, onto the tray (or in the caddy) and push it back in. The drive access light will light for a few seconds, while the software checks what sort of disc you have inserted.

Once the access light has gone out, you can read data from the CD-ROM. If you are in DOS, you can switch to the CD-ROM drive by entering the command 'D:'. If you are in Windows, start the File Manager from the Main group. Above the list of files displayed in File Manager is a row of drive icons. You should see a new icon with the drive D: label beneath it. Click on this to access the CD-ROM.

Tip

If you want to play an AVI file, or a sound or MIDI file, just double-click on the file name and Windows will automatically start the Media Player utility and load the file.

② Click on D:

Basic steps

❑ **To copy from a CD-ROM to the hard disk**

1 Load the CD-ROM, printed side up into the drive, close the tray and wait till the access light is off

2 Start **File Manager** and click on the D: drive icon above the list of files

3 File Manager displays a list of directories and files stored on the CD-ROM

4 Locate the file you want to copy, click on it once and drag the file up and onto the icon for the C: drive (your hard disk)

5 File Manager will check that you want to copy the file to the C: drive. Click the **OK** button to confirm your actions.

Basic steps

❏ **To find a file**

1 Select the D: drive icon

2 Select the **File–Search** menu option

3 Enter the name of the file, or use a wildcard search pattern to find a group of related files. For example, to find all video files you would use '*.AVI'; to find all sound files you would use '*.WAV'

4 Click **OK** and after a few moments, File Manager will display a list of matching files

Take note

If you insert an audio CD or have the CD-ROM in upside down, File Manager will display an error message that there's no disc in the drive.

Searching for files on a CD-ROM

One of the small problems with a CD-ROM is that it can store so much data - over 650Mb. If you are accessing a CD-ROM packed with hundreds of clip-art files, then you will probably spend a long time searching through the directories for the one you want.

File Manager includes a simple search function that's very useful when you're trying to find one file out of hundreds on a CD-ROM.

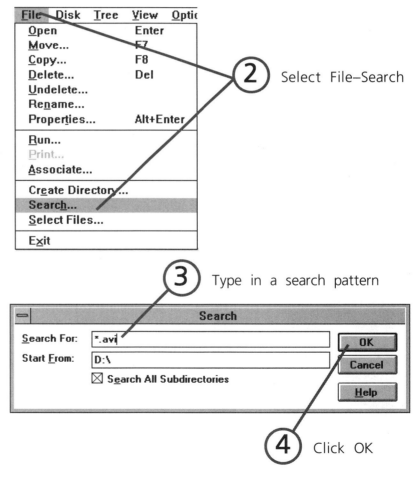

② Select File–Search

③ Type in a search pattern

④ Click OK

Commercial CD-ROMs

So far in this book, you've seen how multimedia works, and later you'll see how to create your own multimedia books. There are also thousands of commercial titles available that will run on your PC. When you bought your PC or CD-ROM drive (if you upgraded) you might have been given a free CD-ROM to get you started.

There is such a wide range, it's difficult to mention all of them. There are exciting games that use video, stereo sound and images to create a virtual world. Encyclopaedias are also popular, and might include text, sound, and images to bring the subject alive.

> **Tip**
>
> Learning becomes more interesting with multimedia. There are several language courses available that feature a video clip of your teacher, with spoken words.

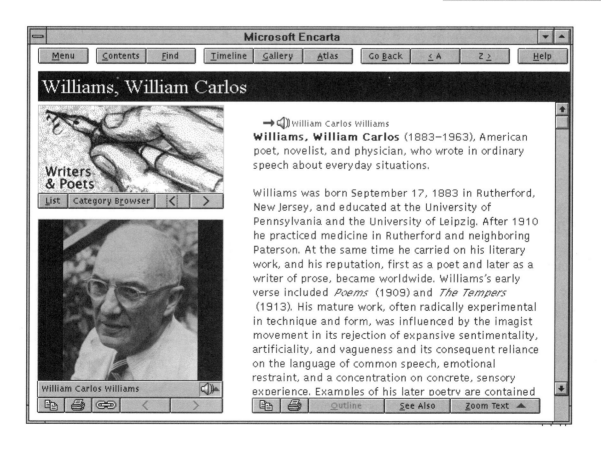

Mozart's World
A Prisoner in Salzburg

The Mozart who, at age 14, had received the Order of the Golden Spur from the Pope, found the provincial atmosphere of Salzburg increasingly stifling. He longed for a job in a more challenging environment. In 1777, the 21–year–old Mozart demanded his release from the service of the Archbishop Hieronymous Colleredo. ▶

Mozart with the Order of the Golden Spur, anonymous, 1777
Scala/Art Resource, New York

Play through

Play this page

Pause

Microsoft Encarta is an encyclopedia that is up-dated each year. It includes text, images, sound and video clips.
(See illustration opposite)

> ## Tip
>
> **Whenever you try out a multimedia title, look carefully to see how the developer created the software. It'll give you plenty of ideas of new ways to create your own.**

Multimedia titles include reference works such as **Microsoft Mozart** – this includes MIDI files that you can play back to hear his music – together with anotation and images.

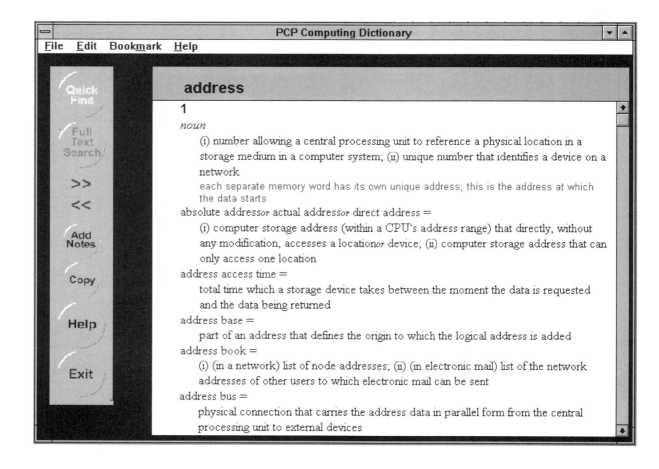

PCP Computing Dictionary

<u>F</u>ile   <u>E</u>dit   Book<u>m</u>ark   <u>H</u>elp

Quick Find

Full Text Search

>>

<<

Add Notes

Copy

Help

Exit

address

1

noun

(i) number allowing a central processing unit to reference a physical location in a storage medium in a computer system; (ii) unique number that identifies a device on a network

each separate memory word has its own unique address; this is the address at which the data starts

absolute address*or* actual address*or* direct address =

(i) computer storage address (within a CPU's address range) that directly, without any modification, accesses a location*or* device; (ii) computer storage address that can only access one location

address access time =

total time which a storage device takes between the moment the data is requested and the data being returned

address base =

part of an address that defines the origin to which the logical address is added

address book =

(i) (in a network) list of node addresses; (ii) (in electronic mail) list of the network addresses of other users to which electronic mail can be sent

address bus =

physical connection that carries the address data in parallel form from the central processing unit to external devices

Titles such as this computer dictionary from PCP squeeze the entire text of a large book into a CD-ROM and include links between words, as well as having search functions.

88

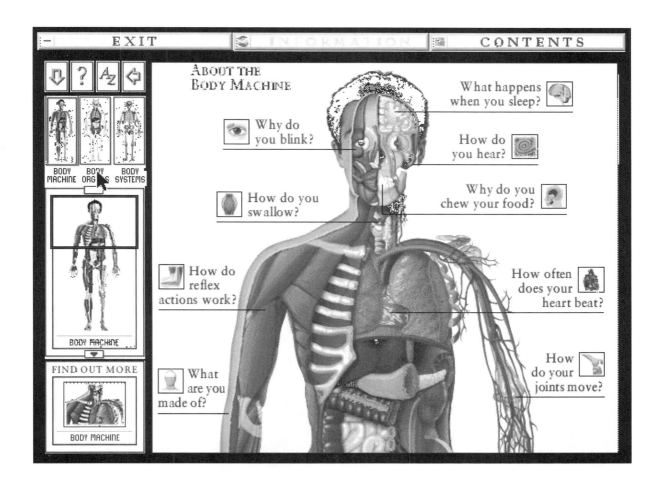

Dorling Kindersley's "How the Human
Body Works" uses hotspots (see page 93)
to link graphics and text to great effect.

Installing CD-ROMs

When you buy a program on a CD-ROM, you will need to install and set it up before it will work properly. For Windows software the convention is to run a little utility called Setup that's stored on the CD-ROM. This copies configuration files onto your hard disk and creates a new program group and icon.

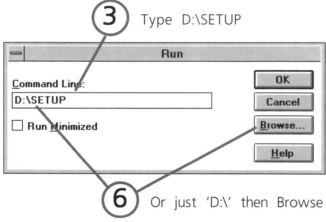

③ Type D:\SETUP

⑥ Or just 'D:\' then Browse

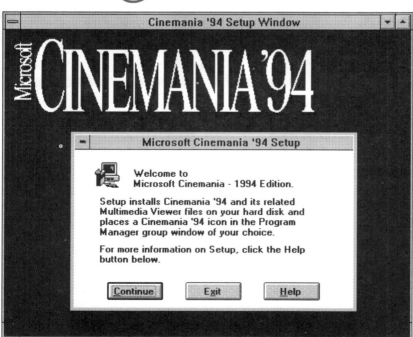

1 Ensure the CD-ROM is in the drive and the access light is not lit

2 Select the File–Run menu option from Program Manager

3 Type in 'D:\setup' – change the drive letter to suit your PC – and click **OK**

4 The setup program should start and install the software onto your hard disk

5 If it doesn't work, the program is called something other than 'setup'. Look in the manual – it could be called 'install'.

6 If this is no help, use **File–Run**, type in the drive letter and select the Browse button

7 From the list of files available on the CD-ROM, pick the install program and click OK

90

Limited installations

Some installation programs give you a choice: either copy the files onto your hard disk, which takes up a lot of disk space, or keep them mostly on the CD-ROM disc, which means that access to the files is slower.

- If you don't use the software very often, choose the second option or you'll use up all your free disk space.

- If the software runs very slowly, try re-installing it onto your hard disk which will be much faster.

Take note

When you install an application, only a small part of the software will be copied onto your hard disk. Most of the files will still be on the CD-ROM, so you will normally have to keep it in the drive when you run the program.

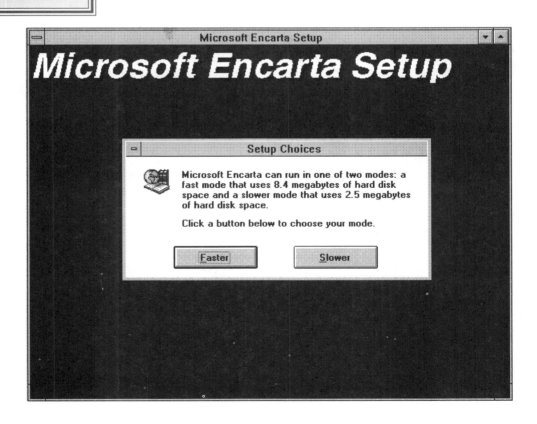

Hypertext

Trying to use a new multimedia title for the first time is not as difficult as it might seem. All titles have similar functions and follow similar conventions for the user-interface (the part of the software that you see).

The design of a screen might be very complex, fancy or very stark, but the way in which you interact with the software is unlikely to vary.

If there's any text on screen, you might see certain words displayed in a different colour or underlined. These are *hot-words*, and they have *hypertext* links to other information. This could be as simple as a little box that pops up to explain a complex term, or it could take you to a different page in the title.

Basic steps

1 Look for hot-words – those that are underlined or displayed in a different colour

2 Move the pointer over the word - it should change shape to look like a hand

3 With the hand pointer over the hot-word, click once on the left button and see what is linked to the word.

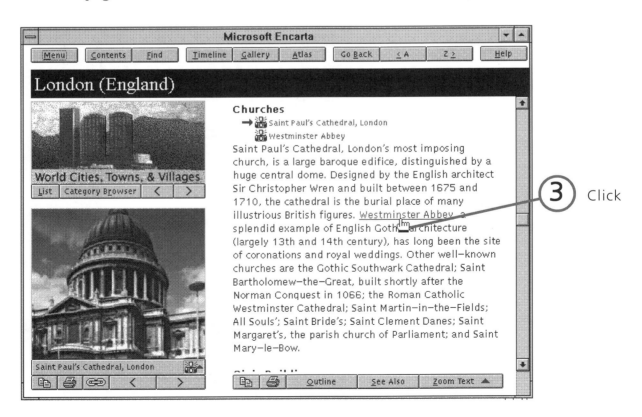

③ Click

Basic steps

1 Move your pointer over a picture and see if the pointer changes shape.

2 If it changes to a hand, you are over a hotspot. This could be part of a picture or an entire picture.

3 When you are over a hotspot, click once with the left button to start the action

Hotspots

A *hotspot* is very similar to a hot-word, but is an area of a picture. For example, if you have a multimedia title describing a violin, the image of the violin might be a hotspot. When you click on the violin, it carries out some action: maybe playing a violin sound, or displaying more detailed information.

② Look for the hand pointer

Take note

Hotspots are not necessarily easy to see. Watch for the hand pointer.

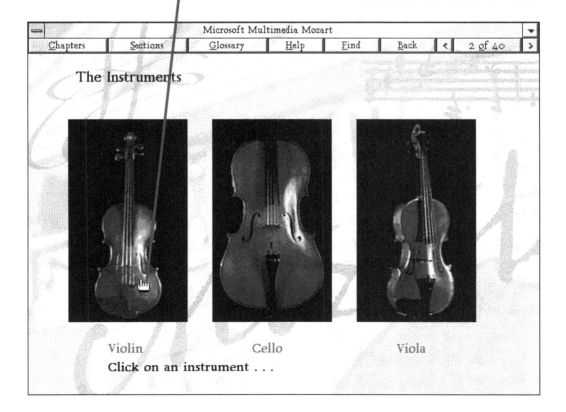

Violin   Cello   Viola

Click on an instrument . . .

Buttons

Buttons are an obvious way of interacting with a multimedia application. They normally have a caption on them that tells you what the button will do. You might be used to normal, grey square buttons in Windows, but a button in a multimedia application can be any shape or colour.

If the multimedia application has a very modern design, there might not be any caption text on the button, instead it might just have a symbol. Some symbols are easy to recognise from other Windows applications:

 open a file

 search

other symbols are not so common:

 to exit the software

 move to the next page in the multimedia book

❑ **To select a button**

1 Look for a 3-D effect shape with caption text or a symbol

2 Move the pointer over the caption or symbol – it might change shape to look like a hand

3 With the hand pointer over the button, click once on the left mouse button and you will start the action

Tip

Some programs, if you move the pointer over the button and wait a couple of seconds, display a tiny caption for the button. Other programs will display a description in a status bar if you click on the right mouse button while pointing at a screen button.

Searching

If the multimedia software contains information, rather than being just a game, you will almost certainly be able to search the file for key words. There are different ways of starting the search function: some programs will use a button, others a menu option.

Once you have opened the search window, you can either type in a word you want to find, or a more complex search sentence. For a simple search, just enter the word and click on OK. For more complex searches, you can use special words called logical operators. These are: AND, OR, NOT and are used between words.

For example, if you want to search for any page that has the words 'mouse' and 'cheese' you would type in:

'mouse AND cheese'.

If you want to make the search more specific, perhaps to exclude any pages that also have the word 'cat', then you would type in

'mouse AND cheese NOT cat'.

Tip

A full-text search lets you search for words in any text stored, but is much slower than searching through a list of keywords.

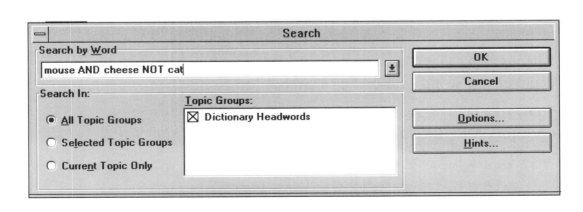

Summary

- Your CD-ROM drive will normally appear as drive D: under **File Manager**

- Use the **File–Search** menu option of File Manager to find files on a CD-ROM

- There are thousands of **commercial titles** available from games to clip-art, teaching, encylopaedias and dictionaries. Look at how they were designed to get ideas for your own production.

- When you **install the software**, some files are copied to your hard disk (for speed), but the bulk remain on the CD-ROM

- When you **run the software**, you normally have to keep the CD-ROM in the drive

- **Hot-words** are used to link to another page or display extra information. They are displayed in a different colour. The pointer changes to a hand when over a hot-word

- **Hotspots** are similar to hot-words, but are parts of an image

- **Buttons** might look like normal Windows buttons or could be any shape with text or a symbol

- To narrow down a **search**, use the special logical operators AND, OR, NOT.

9 Creating Multimedia

Multimedia data

Now that you have explored how multimedia works, you can start to use it to make your everyday documents, memos and messages rather more exciting. This chapter shows you how to use the tools provided with Windows to add sound to a memo and a video clip to a catalogue.

These are simple but very effective uses of multimedia. For special presentations, you could use the multimedia functions built into Windows, but these are not very sophisticated – if you plan to carry out a lot of presentations, you should consider buying special presentation software, as described on page 109.

Take note

To create multimedia applications, you need an authoring package, that lets you create hotspots, hot-words and links to other pages. Many packages make it easy to let your creativity loose.

Basic steps

❑ **to add a sound**

1 Run **Write** and start typing your memo

2 When you reach the point where you want to add a sound, switch back to the Program Manager and start **Sound Recorder**

3 Load the sound file using **File–Open** or record a new comment

Cont...

Windows includes a very powerful feature called OLE (object linking and embedding). This allows any Windows application to use data from almost any other Windows application. For example, if you are typing a memo in Write, you can insert an object created with the Sound Recorder.

It's a great way of livening up a memo or of adding personal spoken notes to explain a spreadsheet or meeting. Of course, you cannot print a sound! So this method works best if you have a network to distribute your files or can send a memo via electronic mail.

① Start Write

② Leave the cursor where the sound will go

Take Note

Any other user can open the Write document and listen to the sound file by double-clicking on the microphone icon.

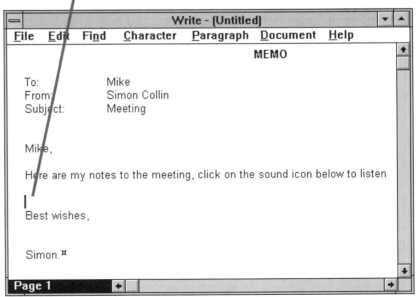

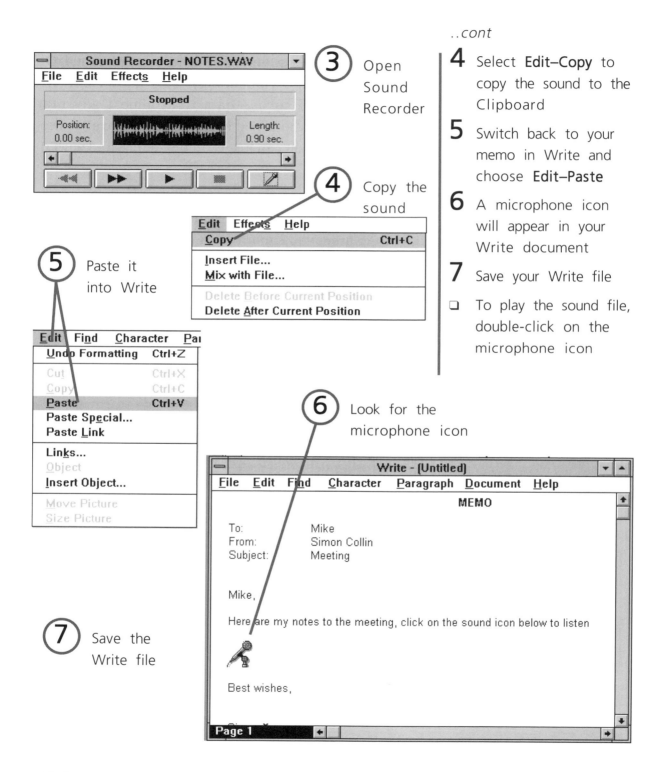

..cont

3 Open Sound Recorder

4 Copy the sound

5 Paste it into Write

6 Look for the microphone icon

7 Save the Write file

4 Select **Edit–Copy** to copy the sound to the Clipboard

5 Switch back to your memo in Write and choose **Edit–Paste**

6 A microphone icon will appear in your Write document

7 Save your Write file

❑ To play the sound file, double-click on the microphone icon

Adding a picture to text

1 Start the Write program

2 Type the letter then position the cursor after the last line

3 Select the **Edit–Insert Object** menu option

4 Scroll through the list of OLE objects until you see Paintbrush

You've seen how to copy and paste a sound into a memo. Using this technique, you can add a picture to a letter. It might be a company logo at the top, or your signature at the bottom of a form letter used for a mail-shot.

To show how to add a picture we will use a slightly different method to that described before. With the sound file, the sound was *copied* to the Clipboard, then *pasted* into the memo. This time, we will *embed* our logo in the letter. The result is the same, but the route is different.

Painting your signature is easy with the Windows Paintbrush program (see page 55 for more on Paintbrush).

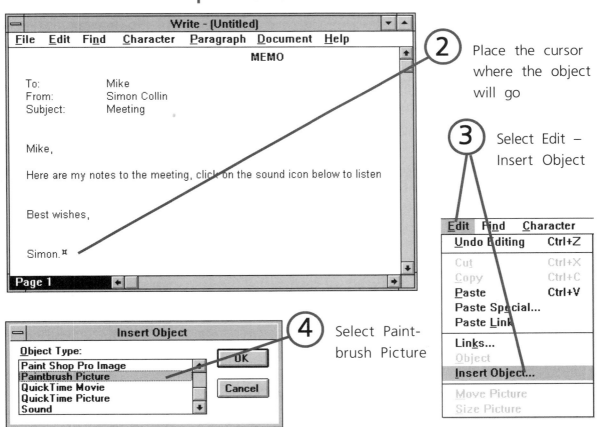

2 Place the cursor where the object will go

3 Select Edit – Insert Object

4 Select Paintbrush Picture

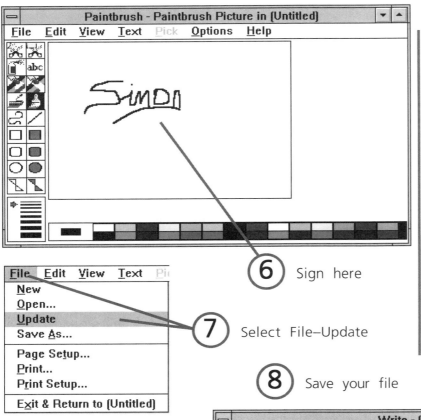

...cont

5 Highlight this option and click **OK**. Windows will automatically start Paintbrush

6 'Sign' your name in Paintbrush using the mouse

7 When you're happy with the result, select the **File–Update** menu option to transfer the image into your letter

8 Back in Write, save your letter

⑥ Sign here

⑦ Select File–Update

⑧ Save your file

Tip

If you want to edit the signature at any time, just double-click on the picture within Write and Windows will automatically start Paintbrush and load the picture of your signature.

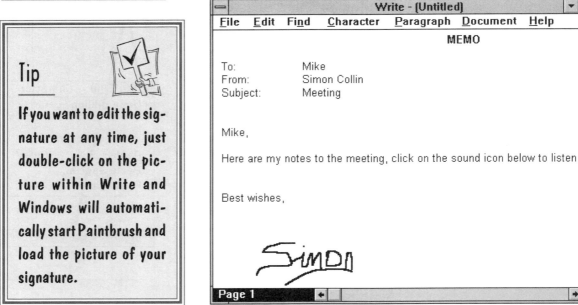

102

Basic steps

An interactive catalogue

1 Start Write – this text will be the foundation for the multimedia objects

2 Type in the basic text for the catalogue and format the heading.

3 Position the cursor at the top of the page, where you will add your company logo

4 Select **Edit–Insert Object** and scroll through the list till you reach Paintbrush, click **OK**

If you put together all the elements you've learnt so far in this chapter you can make an eye-catching catalogue that combines video, sound and pictures. All this through the simple Windows Write program, which means you can experiment with multimedia without having to spend any more money on expensive development software.

To create the catalogue, we will use the OLE functions described in the last few pages. When you added your signature to the letter you will have seen the list of possible multimedia objects that you can embed within Write - and this is exactly how we'll add the video clips.

> **Take note**
>
> When you are creating text with Write, you can use any available fonts from the Character–Fonts menu option.

③ Position the cursor

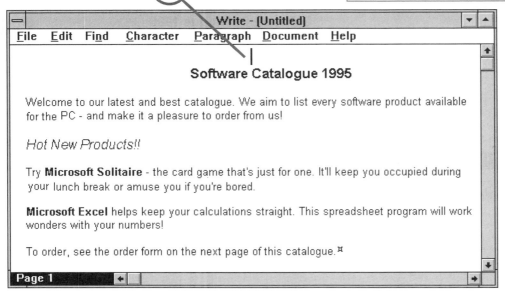

Write - [Untitled]

File Edit Find Character Paragraph Document Help

Software Catalogue 1995

Welcome to our latest and best catalogue. We aim to list every software product available for the PC - and make it a pleasure to order from us!

Hot New Products!!

Try **Microsoft Solitaire** - the card game that's just for one. It'll keep you occupied during your lunch break or amuse you if you're bored.

Microsoft Excel helps keep your calculations straight. This spreadsheet program will work wonders with your numbers!

To order, see the order form on the next page of this catalogue.

Page 1

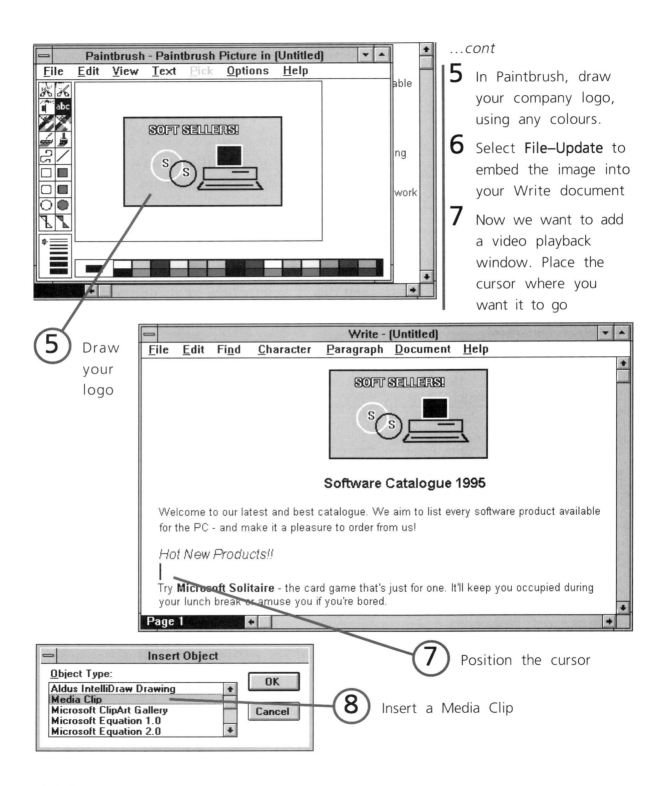

...cont

5 In Paintbrush, draw your company logo, using any colours.

6 Select **File–Update** to embed the image into your Write document

7 Now we want to add a video playback window. Place the cursor where you want it to go

⑤ Draw your logo

⑦ Position the cursor

⑧ Insert a Media Clip

104

...cont

8 Select **Edit–Insert Object**, then **Media Clip** and click **OK**

9 In Media Player, select **File–Open** to load your video clip

10 Choose **File–Update** to transfer this back to your Write document

11 Save your document as 'catalog.wri'

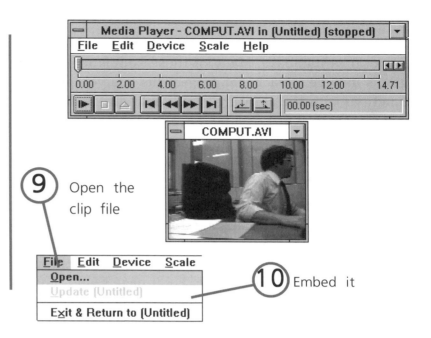

(9) Open the clip file

(10) Embed it

Windows adds a control bar to the clip – any user can click this to plays the video

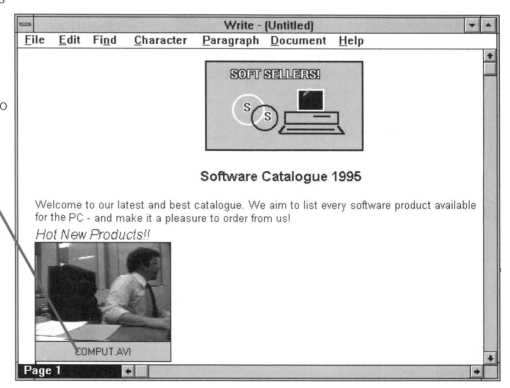

Advanced applications

Most users have a wordprocessor, such as Microsoft Word, or a database. Many of these sophisticated programs include a macro language. This lets you program functions into the software. You could create a special order form in Word or a fax cover sheet. Write doesn't have one, so you can't do anything too clever with it, but with the language of your word-processor, you can create complex multimedia applications.

Most macro languages let you add buttons to a document and also move between pages. If you link these two features together, you can mimic the functions of a multimedia authoring tool and let your users move through pages by clicking on a button. Each page could have a picture of a different product or a video or sound clip.

1 Create a two page document

2 Move to page 2

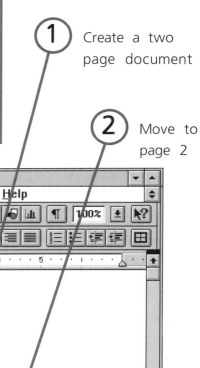

Basic steps

❏ **Authoring in Word**

1 Create two pages of text, add gráphic images or embed video clips

2 Move to the second page

3 Select the **Edit--Bookmark** function

4 Type in 'page2' as the bookmark name and click **Add**

cont...

Take note

This example will work with Microsoft Word for Windows. If you use a different Windows word-processor, check which commands it uses to add a bookmark and move between pages.

Using MS-Word

The pages are each given a unique bookmark which identifies them to Word. Its macro language includes the '*gotobutton*' command. This will create a hot-word that, when selected, will move the user to the named bookmark.

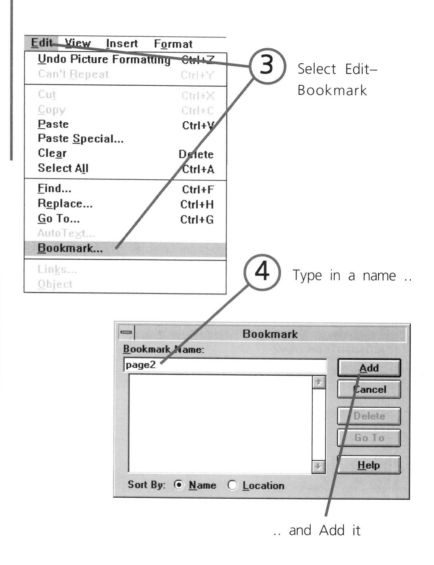

③ Select Edit–Bookmark

④ Type in a name ..

.. and Add it

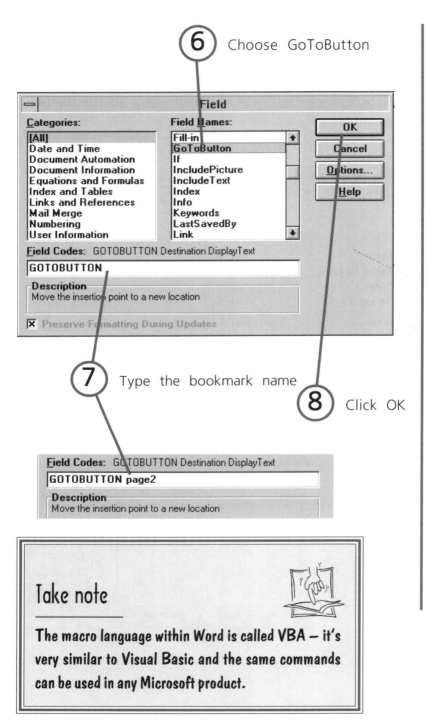

⑥ Choose GoToButton

Field

Categories:

[All]
Date and Time
Document Automation
Document Information
Equations and Formulas
Index and Tables
Links and References
Mail Merge
Numbering
User Information

Field Names:

Fill-in
GoToButton
If
IncludePicture
IncludeText
Index
Info
Keywords
LastSavedBy
Link

OK
Cancel
Options...
Help

Field Codes: GOTOBUTTON Destination DisplayText

GOTOBUTTON

Description
Move the insertion point to a new location

☒ Preserve Formatting During Updates

⑦ Type the bookmark name

Field Codes: GOTOBUTTON Destination DisplayText

GOTOBUTTON page2

Description
Move the insertion point to a new location

⑧ Click OK

Take note

The macro language within Word is called VBA – it's very similar to Visual Basic and the same commands can be used in any Microsoft product.

... cont

5 Move to the first page, position the cursor where you want the button and select the **Insert–Field** menu option

6 Scroll down through the list on the right and choose **GoToButton**

7 In the field below the lists, enter 'page2' afollowing the GOTOBUTTON command,

8 Click **OK**

❑ The bookmark will be displayed on page one of your document; when a user double-clicks on the word, he will be moved to the bookmark 'page2' that is on the second page, effectively turning over a page.

General rules

□ When designing a presentation follow these simple rules to make it as clear and effective as possible.

1 Try and **use a uniform background** to all your slides. Add your logo to reinforce the company image

2 **Don't use too many different typefaces**, no more than two changes per slide

3 **Don't have more than five lines of text** on points for any slide, or your audience will get bored

4 **Make graphs simple and clea**r, two simple graphs are better than one complex

5 **Don't use too many colours or special effects** and try and maintain consistent look to each slide

6 **Print out copies** to give to your audience

Creating a presentation

Presentations are an everyday event in business. An effective presentation is essential when pitching for a new account, displaying sales figures or company results. There are dozens of special software packages that will simplify the task of creating business presentations.

Any presentation is made up of separate *slides*. Each slide on your PC can include text, graphics or graphs.

Typically, you would start with a title slide, then move to the next slide with the contents of the talk and then show slides of figures, graphs or important points.

Presentation software is now very advanced and lets you create a master slide for the entire show. This might have your company logo in one corner and perhaps a uniform background picture or colour. Each separate slide is then created from your existing database. To help your audience, you can print out the slides so that they can make notes and keep a record of your talk.

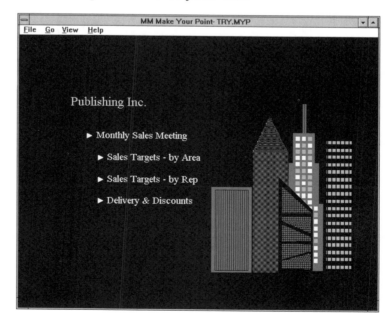

Using Presentation software

Presentation software provides all the functions you need to prepare professional-looking slides. The software should combine a paint-package with simple multimedia functions. To start your presentation, define the 'master' slide. This is the background that will be used for all the slides throughout your presentation. You could draw your company's logo using the paint software.

Once you have the master slide, type in the text for your presentation. If you need to use data from a spreadsheet (to show company results), the presentation software will let you import the data and create a graph.

The finished sequence of slides can be viewed as a slide show. You can set the presentation software to either display each slide for a fixed time before moving onto the next slide, or you can move on one slide by clicking the mouse button.

Tip

Remember to use the spell-check feature of your presentation software - there's nothing worse that mistakes in your presentation!

Presentation software normally includes a wide range of templates to save you time.

Authoring software

The greatest challenge, and the best way of displaying your creative talents, is to develop your own multimedia title. This is not as difficult as you might think and with a little effort and a good idea, you can rival many commercial CD-ROMs.

Up until now, you have tried creating a multimedia catalogue using the tools supplied with Windows. However, Write is not flexible nor powerful enough to manage more complex titles. Your multimedia title will probably have dozens of different pages, images, text, audio and perhaps video clips combining together. Just like a commercial application, you will have to program hotspots, hotwords and buttons that a user can use to move between pages and get the most from your title.

To create a multimedia title you will need to use an authoring package. There are many different types available that vary in price and how difficult they are to learn. Surprisingly, some of the cheapest are also the simplest to use - mainly because they don't have hundreds of complex features that only a programmer could use.

Types of packages

There are two types of authoring package. One uses a *script language* in which the developer (you) write out instructions to place images and video clips on a page and define how they react to a user. These types of product are powerful because a programmer can do just about anything with them - but they are very difficult to learn. It's just like learning a whole new language.

Take note

If you want to distribute or sell your new multimedia title to other users, some authoring packages charge a fee, others let you do this for free.

The second type of authoring package is *icon-based*. These are often just as powerful as a script-based package, but are much simpler for a non-programmer to use. Any action is represented by an icon. You create pages by dragging your images and text onto the page and then you can define how they react to a user with the action icons. In short, you don't need to be able to program, only to be able to click and drag icons.

Designing a title

To create your own multimedia title using an icon-based authoring package is easy – but you have to plan ahead carefully to avoid problems.

Basic steps

1 Sketch the layout of each page in the book

2 Compile a list of all the resources you need: the text, images, sounds, icons, and video clips

3 Record all the sounds, edit them and add any special effects

4 Create the graphics

5 Type in the text and note where you want to include hot-words

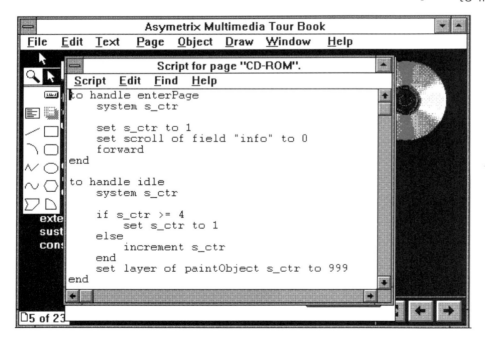

You create a title in Multimedia Toolbook by writing a script

112

6 Use the authoring software to design the pages, include the buttons to move between the pages

7 Import and place the sounds, images and text you've prepared

8 Use the authoring functions to define how the title reacts to the user's actions

9 Sit back and play your finished title

Icon Author lets you design a title by linking icons – a different method to Toolbook.

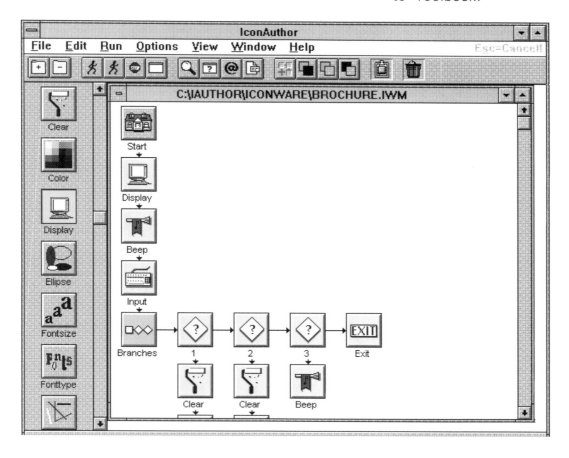

Summary

❏ You can include **images, sound or video clips** in almost any Windows application to add sparkle to a document

❏ Once you have embedded sound or video in a document, **any other user can see the video** or listen to the sound

❏ Use the **macro language** of your wordprocessor to create separate pages and move between them

❏ Presentations look professional if you use **presentation software** and stick to simple rules

❏ **Authoring packages** allow you to develop your own multimedia title with little programming

10 Tuning Windows

Tuning for Multimedia

Multimedia is very demanding on all the elements in your PC - both hardware and software. A short video clip can take several megabytes of disk space and sound and images can soon fill up your hard disk. When you start to edit images or manipulate them with presentation software or an authoring package, you'll find that your PC is pushed to its limits.

Over the next few pages, you'll see how to tune Windows so that multimedia applications run faster and more smoothly

Before you start to tune Windows and setup your PC to its optimum configuration, gather together the basic information about what it has installed: the size of hard disk, amount of RAM, video display, speed of the CD-ROM drive and so on. Lastly, it's worth checking how well Windows is currently setup to see how efficiently it is running before you start making changes.

❑ **To check disk space**

1 Start **File Manager** from the **Main** program group

2 Click on the **C: drive** icon for your hard disk

3 The **free disk space** is displayed in the bottom left-hand corner. Beside this is the **total disk space** for your hard disk

(1) Run File Manager

File Manager

(2) Select C:

File   Disk   Tree

C: [As

a   c   d

├ ☐ plants
├ ☐ psfonts

(3) Check free space

├ ☐ viewer
├ ☐ wgpo0000
├ ☐ windows
│ └ ☐ anw_data
☐ comp
☐ encar
☐ ger_d

C: 73.0MB free, 404MB total

Take note

If you want to know how to check the amount of RAM memory, turn to page 22.

Basic steps

❏ **To check your screen resolution**

1 Double-click on the **Windows Setup** icon in the Main group

2 The current screen resolution will be displayed under the **Display** setting, make a note of the figures

3 Select **File–Exit** to leave making any changes

❏ **To check Windows efficiency**

1 Select the **Help–About Program Manager** menu option from **Program Manager**

2 Make a note of the last setting, percentage system resources free.

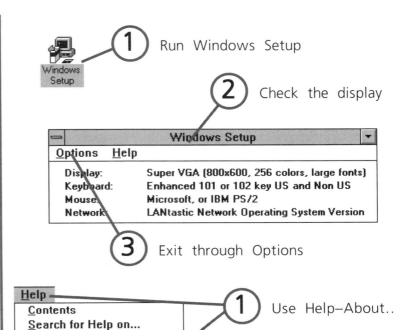

1 Run Windows Setup

2 Check the display

3 Exit through Options

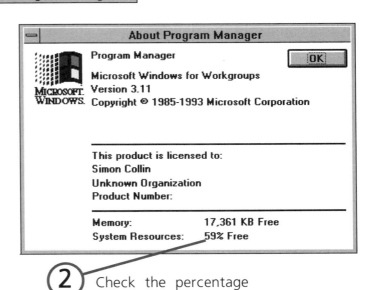

1 Use Help–About..

2 Check the percentage

117

Configuring memory

One of the most important parts of Windows is its virtual memory. This feature allows Windows to treat part of your hard disk as temporary storage for programs that it cannot fit into RAM. It means that if you only have 4Mb of RAM fitted to your PC, Windows can make it appear as if you have 10Mb by treating 6Mb of hard disk space as *virtual memory* (the term virtual mean imaginary).

The amount of hard disk space used by Windows for virtual memory is called the *Windows swap file*. There are two types of swap file: *temporary* and *permanent*.

- A temporary swap file is set up when you start Windows and deleted when you shut down.

- A permanent swap file is always on the hard disk and is faster than a temporary swap file.

Windows can control some hard disks better than others using a special 32-bit access method. Normally, it transfers data to and from the hard disk 16 bits at a time, but with a compatible hard disk, you can double it to 32-bits.

1 Close all programs so that you only have Program Manager displayed

2 Double-click on the **Control Panel** icon and double-click on the **Enhanced** icon

3 Select the **Virtual Memory** button, then from the next screen select **Change** button

4 From the **Type** selection, choose **Permanent**

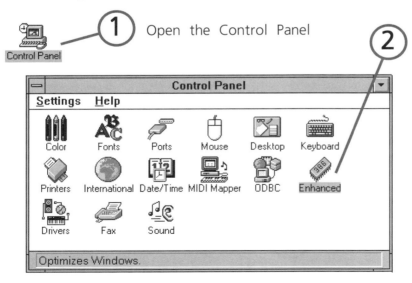

Open the Control Panel

Select Enhanced

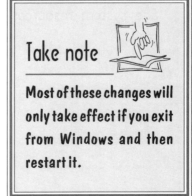

Take note

Most of these changes will only take effect if you exit from Windows and then restart it.

5 Near the bottom of the window, check the recommended size of the swap file and enter this in the New setting if it's not already this figure

6 Select both 32-bit file access and 32-bit disk access

7 Click on the OK button to save any changes

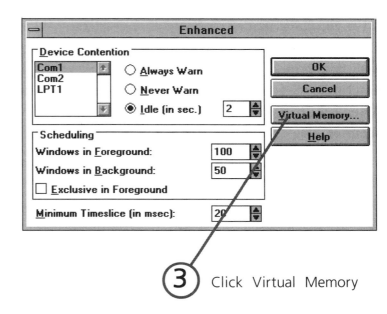

③ Click Virtual Memory

④ Choose Permanent

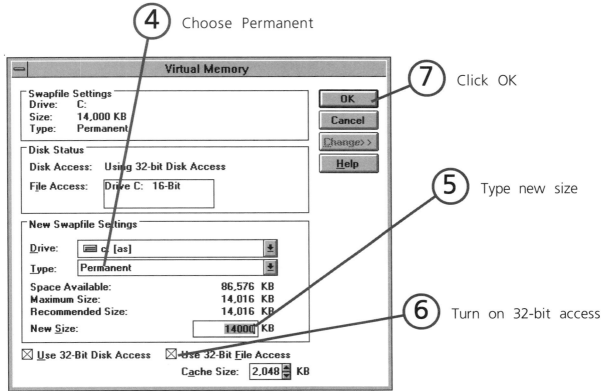

⑦ Click OK

⑤ Type new size

⑥ Turn on 32-bit access

Setting up DOS

After you have made the basic changes to the Windows swap file, you can turn your attention to ensuring that DOS is correctly configured. DOS looks after the basic functions in your PC and runs underneath Windows. When you installed a driver for your CD-ROM drive or scanner, you configured this through DOS.

If your PC has 4Mb of RAM installed, the first 640Kb is set aside for DOS programs. The remainder can be used by Windows applications. Strangely, Windows 3.1 itself is actually a DOS program! To get the best performance out of your PC, the drivers that control your CD-ROM drive, sound card, mouse and so on must be properly configured.

To get the most free memory for DOS you need to load all these drivers into the area above the 640Kb limit. This might sound a strange way of working, but it's steeped in history and it's also possible to configure your PC automatically. DOS comes with a utility called *Memmaker*. Whenever you add a new piece of hardware that needs a software driver, run MemMaker to re-configure your PC to its optimum memory settings.

1 Exit it from Windows completely, don't do this by selecting the **MS-DOS** icon

2 At the C:\> prompt, start Memmaker by typing '**MEMMAKER**' and pressing return

3 If this doesn't work, move to the \DOS directory with the '**CD \DOS**' command, then repeat step 2

4 Memmaker will take you through all the steps, ask you a few simple questions then automatically check all your PC's settings.

Tip

Keep your hard disk in tip-top condition by running the DOS utility *Defrag* regularly. This sorts out all the files stored on the hard disk and puts them in a sensible order so that they can be accessed more rapidly. How long it takes depends on the size of your hard disk, but it could be a couple of hours.

You must exit from Windows before running Defrag.

```
Microsoft MemMaker
_____

  Welcome to MemMaker.

  MemMaker optimizes your system's memory by moving memory-resident
  programs and device drivers into the upper memory area. This
  frees conventional memory for use by applications.

  After you run MemMaker, your computer's memory will remain
  optimized until you add or remove memory-resident programs or
  device drivers. For an optimum memory configuration, run MemMaker
  again after making any such changes.                            o

  MemMaker displays options as highlighted text. (For example, you
  can change the "Continue" option below.) To cycle through the
  available options, press SPACEBAR. When MemMaker displays the
  option you want, press ENTER.

  For help while you are running MemMaker, press F1.

              Continue or Exit? Continue
 ENTER=Accept Selection  SPACEBAR=Change Selection  F1=Help  F3=Exit
```

Above, the introductory screen from Memmaker.
Notice the key prompts in the bottom line.

Below, the Advanced Options screen. When in doubt
about an option, leave it at the default setting.

Tip

For more about configuring
DOS, see the companion book
MS-DOS Made Simple

Change this to Yes
if you use Windows

```
Microsoft MemMaker
_____

                     Advanced Options


  Specify which drivers and TSRs to include in optimization?     No
  Scan the upper memory area aggressively?                       No
  Optimize upper memory for use with Windows?                    No
  Use monochrome region (B000-B7FF) for running programs?        No
  Keep current EMM386 memory exclusions and inclusions?          Yes
  Move Extended BIOS Data Area from conventional to upper memory? Yes
  _____


  To select a different option, press the UP ARROW or DOWN ARROW key.
  To accept all the settings and continue, press ENTER.




 ENTER=Accept All  SPACEBAR=Change Selection  F1=Help  F3=Exit
```

121

Summary

❑ To run multimedia applications your PC needs to be set up correctly and running efficiently

❑ Ensure that the **swap file** is of the correct size and, for top performance, use a permanent swap file

❑ If you hard disk supports it, use **32-bit disk access** to double the rate at which data is transferred

❑ Get the best from your memory by running **Memmaker** when you install new hardware to ensure it's correctly configured

❑ Run **Defrag** on a regular basis to keep the files on your hard disk in order

11 Windows 95

Windows 3.1 and 95

Throughout this book, I have concentrated on using multimedia with Microsoft Windows. This covers Windows 3.x and Windows for Workgroups. These two products will soon be replaced by the new version from Microsoft, called Windows 95. Best of all, Microsoft has improved Windows 95 so that it runs on the same configuration as the current versions of Windows, but it will actually run faster!

Everything you have learnt so far in this book still works for Windows 95. In fact, except for a new 'look' to Windows, which has been given a complete facelift, the basic way of using the software is still the same. In this chapter I'll show you the new tools and utilities and how they compare to the similar programs included with the current version of Windows 3.1.

Tip

Windows 95 has a new front-end that makes it easier for new users to get to grips with Windows.

Clicking a top level icon opens up its window

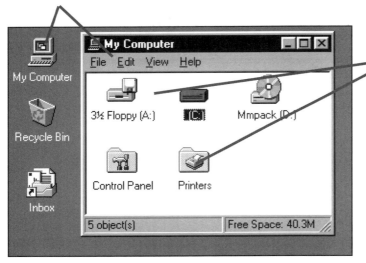

Within the same window you can have access to disk drives – as through the old FIle Manager – and to program groups – as through the old PRogram Manager

Paint 95

Windows 95 includes many similar programs that you already know from the current version of Windows – such as Paint. However, the new version of Paint is much improved and gives you far better control when drawing pictures, including more advanced palette control – using a tool to 'pick up' a colour from the image and transfer it to the palette

Take note

WIndows 95 has improved on the Paint utility to include a Help bar (bottom line), together with a co-ordinate display and more powerful editing functions.

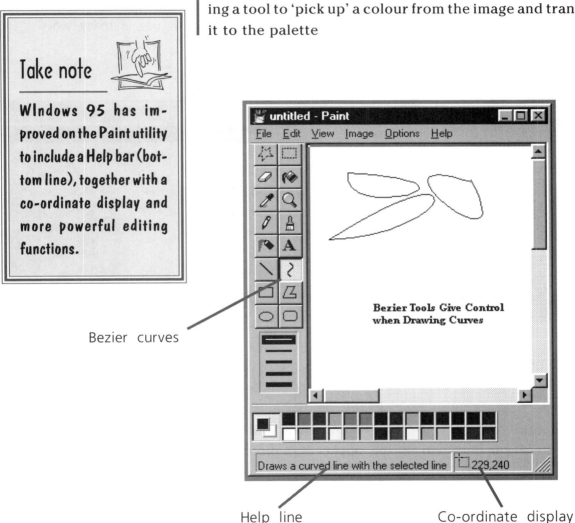

Bezier curves

Help line

Co-ordinate display

125

Starting Utilities

In the current version of Windows 3.x, all the basic utilities are in one of two groups: Main or Accessories. In addition, you can configure the setup through the Control Panel icon. In Windows 95, this has changed radically. To start a utility, such as Media Player or Sound Recorder, you select the option from a menu then click the button in the bottom left-hand corner of the screen called, appropriately, Start!

After you have got over the initial shock of the new screen layout and design, you should find Windows 95 even easier to use in many ways.

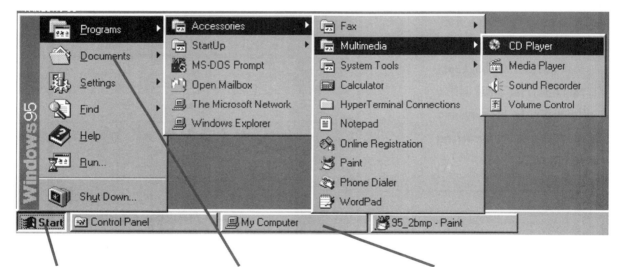

Instead of organising programs in groups, there is a more fluid menu system, with instant access to any utilities and other programs through the Start button.

Windows 95 makes it easier to start working directly on documents, rather than having to run the application program first.

You can switch between currently active folders and programs by clicking on a button in the bar at the bottom of the screen.

Multimedia utilities

Take note

Windows 95 has better support for AVI files - the standard format for video clips - and so playback is much smoother than on the current version of Windows.

Windows 95 has a very similar range of multimedia utilities to the current version including Sound Recorder and Media Player. It also has CD Player, a dedicated utility to play Audio CDs, so you no longer need to use the Media Player utility. With the CD Player, you can give each CD a description and Windows 95 will store this and display it the next time you play that particular CD.

CD Player

This new utility lets you play any audio CD and define the track order and the name of the CD.

Media Player

This utility is still the main way of playing audio, video or MIDI files.

Sound Recorder

This allows you to record and play back WAV files.

Configuring Hardware

Setting up the multimedia hardware in your PC is much easier under Windows 95. Instead of having to struggle with the Drivers icon in the Control Panel, Windows 95 can automatically detect and install new hardware for you. For more advanced users, there is direct support for different monitor types to get the best colour display.

Take note

If your Windows 95 screen does not look like this, don't worry. Microsoft has separated out the networking and some of the other more complex functions into add-on 'bonus packs'. This does not affect Multimedia.

If you're keen on games, you can configure a joystick.

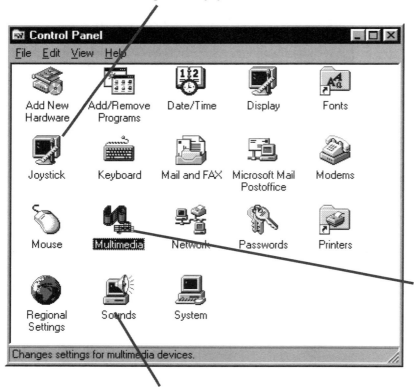

The properties of all the multimedia add-ons in your PC can be configured from one icon in the Control Panel.

The sounds icon, as in Windows 3.1, assigns sounds to events.

The Multimedia icon

Within Control Panel there are many new icons, but the most important for this book is the Multimedia icon. This displays all the details of the sound card, video capture, and MIDI ports that you have installed in your PC. If you look at the top of the window, you'll see page 'tabs'; if you click on these, they will display the configuration details of the particular piece of multimedia hardware.

Tabs to turn to other multimedia control pages

Graphic prompts and control are used wherever possible

The drop down lists include all the popular (and many of the less common) devices currently in use

If you have unusual requirements, you can customise the system to suit

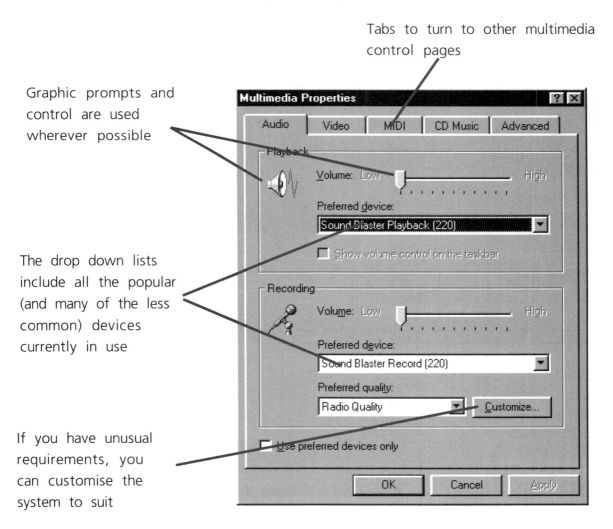

129

Wizards

Adding new hardware is very easy under Windows 95 thanks to a new feature called *Wizards*. These are little utilities that try and automate the process of installing new hardware. For example, if you add a sound card, when you next switch on your PC, Windows 95 will detect that there's a new piece of hardware installed and will start the New Hardware Wizard. This takes you through the setup and configuration process step by step.

A Wizard will sometimes prompt you for information or give you a chance to specify a setting, but most of them can do their job so well that all you have to do is click Next!

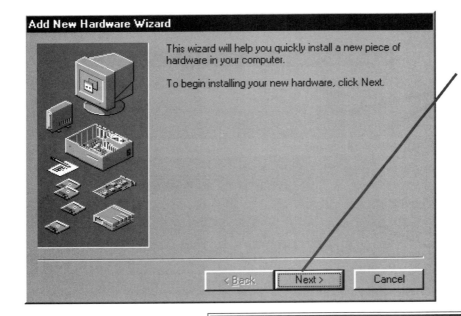

Add New Hardware Wizard

This wizard will help you quickly install a new piece of hardware in your computer.

To begin installing your new hardware, click Next.

< Back   Next >   Cancel

Take note

Plug and Play is a new feature that will be included in many new PCs. It means that you can plug in any new piece of hardware and Windows 95 will automatically set it up and configure correctly. Until you've got this feature, the Wizards help you out.

Setting properties

Once you have installed new hardware, perhaps a new video display adapter, you can see exactly how it is setup and you can change any setting through its 'properties' page – here is the setup for the video display in my PC and the options that I can change.

Click a tab to get to other aspects of the display

The preview shows the effects of your settings, to give you a chance to change your mind before you OK the new display

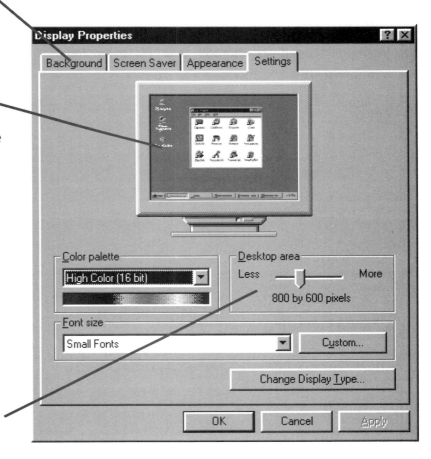

The settings include the size of the Desktop area, as well as the more expected choice of colour palettes and font sizes.

Summary

❑ **Windows 95** is the new version that replaces Windows 3.x and Windows for Workgroups.

❑ It includes **good support for all the multimedia** functions covered in this book

❑ Many of the **utilities** are still called the same, but their functions may have been enhanced

❑ **Installing** new multimedia hardware is much simpler with the help of the **Wizards**

❑ You **don't need to upgrade your PC** to install Windows 95

Glossary

Glossary

Adapter card

Flat board with electronic components that fits into an expansion slot in your PC; used to add a feature, such as a CD-ROM controller

Analogue signal

Signal that is continuously variable, such as speech; a PC has to convert analogue signals into numeric form before it can process them

Analog to digital conversion

Process of changing an analog signal (such as a voice or music) into a stream of numbers that can then be stored on a computer. The process works by looking at the height of the analog signal several thousand times every second and recording this as a number.

Animation

To display a sequence of drawings each slightly different to give the impression of movement

Authoring package

software that allows you to create your own multimedia titles by controlling images, sound, video and text on screen and define how they react to a user's instructions

AVI (audio/video interleaved)

Method of storing video clips with an audio signal so that it can be played back without special hardware (but it does require a video capture card to record video)

Bit (binary digit)

Smallest piece of data that a computer can handle: can either be 1 or 0; a byte is made up of eight bits

Bitmap

Image in which the colour of each pixel is defined, rather than a vector image in which the coordinates of lines and shapes are described

BMP

Filename extension for the standard way of storing bitmap images

CD-Audio

Standard audio CD that stores music or voice

CD Player

Windows 95 utility that gives you a new and better way of playing audio CDs on a multimedia PC

CD-ROM

Flat, plastic disc that can store around 650Mb of data; the data can be video, sound, text or image data and is read using a laser beam as the disc spins

CD-ROM XA

Standard that defines how a drive reads video and audio at the same time, also used to read PhotoCD discs

Cel

Single image within an animation

Channel

Method of identifying an instrument in a MIDI setup so that it receives the musical notes intended for it

Clip-art

Pre-drawn images that are supplied with a graphics program and can be used to enhance your presentations

Device driver

Special software that controls a piece of hardware, such as a sound card or CD-ROM drive

Dithering

Method of giving the impression of a colour by using a pattern of different coloured pixels that the eye blends together; for example, black and white blend to give the impression of grey. Applied to curves, dithering with a lighter colour can smooth out jagged edges.

Embedding

To include a multimedia object, such as a sound file or image within another Windows application

Expansion bus

Electrical contacts from the computer's processor that allow it to communicate with other electronic devices. For example, inside a PC are several expansion connectors that allow plug-in expansion cards to electrically connect to the computer's processor and memory.

FM synthesizer

One method that a sound card uses to produce sound from MIDI instructions

Frame

A single image that is part of a series that make up a video or animation clip. Full motion video shows smooth movement by displaying around 30 separate frames every second.

Full-motion video

Video that plays back smoothly at around 30 frames every second

Hotspot

Section of an image that is linked to a different page or event; when a user selects the hotspot, it moves them to another page or activates the event

Hot-word

Word displayed in a different colour or underlined that links to a related text, or a different page

Hypertext

Text that contains hot-words that are linked to other sections of text; a user can click on one hot-word and this displays a related piece of text

Interactive multimedia

Multimedia in which the user can explore the data by clicking on hotspots, buttons and hot-words

Interlaced

Method of displaying pictures on a monitor in which the image is built up in two passes. The first pass draws in the every other line on the screen, the second pass fills in the remainder. Most monitors are interlaced.

Interrupt (IRQ)

Electrical signal generated by a sound card, disk drive, MIDI port or other device to tell the computer's processor that it wants to transfer data.

MCI (Multi Channel Interface)

Standard way of controlling multimedia devices from within Windows; MCI defines the instructions used

Media Player

Uutility (in the Accessories group) that can play back sound, video or animation clips

MIDI (Musical Instrument Digital Interface)

Method of linking electronic instruments and HiFi systems to, and controlling them from a PC

Morphing

Software in which the user enters a starting image and a different end image; the software generates an animated sequence that gradually changes the first image to the last

MPC

Standard set of guidelines that a multimedia PC should meet

Multisession

CD-ROM drive and controller that can read data that has been stored on the disc at two or more different times (sessions). For example, if you store some photographs on a PhotoCD, then two weeks later you store some more on the same PhotoCD disc you have created a disc with two sessions. The second session can only be read using a multisession drive.

OLE (Object Linking and Embedding)

Windows function that lets one application use data from a different application; for example, to include a sound sample in a document

Patch

Term used to describe the settings that define the sound a MIDI synthesizer will play on a particular channel.

PhotoCD

Method of storing scanned images of photographs on a CD-ROM; normally produced when your photographs are being developed and read with a CD-ROM XA drive

Pixel (picture element)

Single dot on a screen; the smallest element that can be controlled and recoloured

QuickTime

Method of storing video and animation clips, developed by Apple for the Macintosh but which can be viewed on a PC.

RAM (Random Access Memory)

Short term memory made of electronic chips that can store data while the PC is switched on. They are much faster than a hard disk, but not permanent and more expensive; a PC normally has 4Mb, and can have up to 32Mb fitted

Sampling

Process carried out by an analogue-to-digital converter (such as a sound recorder) in which the analogue signal is examined thousands of times every second and converted into a number

Scanner

Device that lets you turn images on paper into a graphic file that can be used on your PC

SCSI (Small Computer Systems Interface)

A standard for connecting devices such as a CD-ROM drive or scanner to a PC

Sequencer

Software that works like a MIDI recorder. It stores the notes being played on a keyboard or other MIDI instrument onto a disk so that the musician can then display, edit or playback the notes.

SIMM

Small board with several memory chips mounted on it and a connector along the bottom edge. These are the usual way to expand the memory of a computer.

Sound Blaster

Probably the most popular of all the *sound cards* currently on the market, and almost a standard in itself

Sound card

Adapter that fits into an expansion slot and connects to a speaker and microphone and lets you record sound on your hard disk and play it back through the speakers

Sound Recorder

Utility (in the Accessories group) that lets you record, playback or edit sounds

S-VGA (Super VGA)

Current standard for colour graphics displays that can support resolution of up to 800x600 pixels

Synthesizer

Device that can generate sounds in response to data that represents musical notes. Normally, PC sound cards have a synthesizer chip that allows them to generate sounds from MIDI data. see also FM synthesizer

Vector image

Picture that is described with lines and curves that are stored as a series of co-ordinates. This means that the quality of the image remains the same even if you zoom in on an area. Bitmap images, in comparison, store an image by defining each pixel.

VGA (Virtual Graphics Array)

Older standard for colour graphics displays that can support resolutions of up to 640x480 pixels

Video clip

Real-life full-motion action stored on a PC, normally in an AVI format file

Video RAM

Memory on a video adapter card used to store the image displayed on the monitor. If you add more memory to your video adapter you normally boost its ability to display more colours or higher resolution graphics.

WAV file

File format used to store a sound on a PC

Index

Symbols

24-bit colour 54

32-bit access 118

A

Access time 13

Accessories group 30, 55, 73

Adapter card 134

Analog to digital conversion 134

Analogue signal 14, 134

AND 95

Animation 78, 134

Audio CDs 13, 38

Audio Video Interleaved 70

Authoring software 111, 134

AVI files 18, 70, 72, 73, 84, 134

B

Bit 134

Bitmap 134

Bitmap graphic file 64

Bitmap graphic images 52

Black and white scanner 64

BMP 56, 134

Book 3

Buttons 3, 94

C

CD Player 127, 134

CD-Audio 134

CD-ROM 10, 12, 86, 135

CD-ROM drive 10, 12, 22, 84, 116

CD-ROM drive , installation 27

CD-ROM XA 135

CD-ROMs, installing 90

CD-XA 66

Cel 79, 135

Channel 135

Chroma key 71

Clip-art 56, 67, 135

Clipboard 56, 100

Compose 46

Control Panel 24, 41

Cursor shapes 60

D

Darkroom 62

Defrag 120

Device driver 135

Dissolve 77

Dithering 135

Dot-pitch 17

Drawing tools 63

141

Driver software 23

DTP 65

E

Edit-Copy 57, 100

Edit-Paste 57, 100

EDL 76

Embedding 101, 135

Expansion bus 135

Expansion connector 23

Expansion slot 64

F

Fast forward 33, 39

File Manager 8, 84

File-Search 85

Flat-bed scanners 19, 64

FM synthesizer 44, 135

Frame 18, 70, 135

Free disk space 116

Full-motion video 136

G

Graphics Adapter 11, 17

Grey-scale 64

H

Hand-held scanners 19, 64

Headphones 38

HiFi 33, 38

Hook 40

Hot-words 3, 92, 136

Hotlinks 3

Hotspot 136

Hypertext 3, 92, 136

I

Icon 60

Icon-based authoring 112

Install 90

Interactive 5

Interactive multimedia 136

Interlaced 136

Interrupt 23, 136

J

Jack Plug 14

Jagged lines, smoothing 59

K

Keyword search 95

Kodak PhotoCD 66

R

RAM 11, 17, 22, 26, 116, 118, 137

RCA connectors 14

Recording studio 49

Rewind 33

S

S-VGA 11, 17, 54, 138

Sample 34

Sample Rate 15

Sample Size 15

Sampling 15, 137

Scanner 19, 137

Script language 111

SCSI 12, 19, 64, 138

SCSI-2 27

Search, files on a CD-ROM 85

Search, text on CD-ROM 95

Sequence, video 39

Sequencer 44, 46, 49, 138

Setup 90

SIMM 26, 138

Slides 109

SMPTE 76

Sound Blaster 138

Sound card 4, 10, 14, 138

Sound Recorder 7, 30, 32, 40, 99, 138

Sounds, combining 35

Speakers 14

Special effects 37

Start button, Windows 95 126

Swap file 118

Synthesizer 16, 138

synthesizer 44

T

Text search 95

TIFF 52

Tracks 39

Transition 76

Tweening 78

U

upgrade 22

V

VCR 71

Vector graphics 52

Vector image 138

VGA 11, 17, 54, 138

Video 70

Video Cameras 18, 71

Video capture card 18

Video card 71